This Book Belongs To:

_____

What's yours is His ⇄ What's His is *Yours*

GOD
AND THE
G⊙AL
DIGGER

**A 40 Day
Detox-Devotional
for the "Boss" in every woman**

ADRIA BEE

First Edition Copyright © 2019 by Adria Bee

Second Edition Copyright © 2024 by Adria Bee

All rights reserved. Published by CMR Publishers. No part of this book may be reproduced, stored in a retrieval system, or transmitted by any means without the written permission of the author.

Unless stated, scripture quotations are taken from The Holy Bible, New International Version® NIV® Copyright © 1973 1978 1984 2011 by Biblica, Inc. ™ Used by permission. All rights reserved worldwide.

ISBN: 979-8-9873111-4-1

Heartfelt Thanks to:

Mom & Dad: The true leaders of prayer, love and guidance.

Wendell, Kristi, Rashad & Nicole: My biggest supporters and cheerleaders

Kristi Lee Collie: Book Layout Designer and Editor of *God & the GOAL Digger*

Jason T. Bain: Cover Illustrator of *God & the GOAL Digger*

Jerchovia, Rian, Ife, Vernique, Hope (Mom), Ianthia, Nicole and Asline: My first readers and book evaluators

YOU: For taking the time to try out a book from a simple Island girl with big God dreams. I pray that you, Love, will be blessed with joy, peace, adventure, love, open doors and kindness beyond measure in Jesus' name ♥.

And last but *best*,
To my Lord and Savior, *Jesus Christ* - for teaching me that in a world of "can'ts".

I can.

I will.

Adria Bee

To *him*: Thank you for the lessons and the love journey.

Quotes:

"This devotional is such a God-send in the modern era. It is a rich, much-needed mix of faith and the realities of being a woman in the modern age! Praying through issues of expectation, work, friendships and hardships is not only empowering but makes me feel a special bond to anyone reading – we are not alone, and now we have a daily reminder. Thank you, Adria, for such a timely and spirit filled book!"

Jerchovia Z. Moxey | *Marketer, Graphic Designer, Blogger, Miss World New Providence 2019*

"An amazing 40-day devotional! This touches on all aspects of what it means to be a Goal-Digger, with God at the center of it all. From the first day to the absolute last, it feels like a consistent journey that progresses as each day passes, culminating into what feels like the end of a ride you don't want to end. Adria takes us on this incredible personal discovery of ourselves and speaks to struggles we ALL face as women. She provides daily encouragement while using some of her own life experiences as a background. *God and the GOAL Digger* is truly a phenomenal devotional for the everyday phenomenal woman."

Rian A. Sands | *Marketing Brand Manager*

"This book is a remarkable accomplishment for Adria. She went through a transformational year that would have stifled the growth of many. Instead, she courageously channeled her experience into writing this inspirational devotional that will guide other women through their personal journeys. I am honored to have witnessed her evolution as a human, her growth as a woman, the deepening of her faith and the anchoring of her purpose in God. Adria lives and breathes the words on these pages. Her honesty and vulnerability are powerful reminders that sharing our testimonies bring light to this world, uplift the spirits of others and liberate us from our own insecurities. Adria is a true Goal Digger on a mission to unite women across the globe!"

Ife Bethel –Sears | *Entrepreneur*

"A breath of fresh air! Adria, thank you for sharing your words of wisdom and encouragement. Everyone's journey is unique; however, we often face similar challenges, and the solution is simple: Seek God. This 40-day devotion is just what we need to make it through our personal and professional lives."

Vernique Henfield | *Media Correspondent, Accountant*

"I admire Adria's courage to share freely from her heart some of the trials and challenges that have crossed her path. Her use of wit and humor to make a point or introduce a *goal* made me smile and ponder at the same time. I even learned some good chic-tech stuff that I've never even thought of.

I sincerely feel that in *God and the GOAL Digger,* Adria has something special for every woman who reads it – young and old alike. And I am so very proud of my youngest daughter. God bless you, Boo!"

Hope McCardy | *Christian Author, Mother of Adria Bee*

"This book is a beautiful ode to womanhood, spirituality and the art of simply being. I love that it taps into every aspect of what women deal with daily: health, friendship, family, self-esteem and work. A must read for anyone wanting to re-center themselves and go on a journey of self-fulfillment."

Ianthia Ferguson | *Travel Writer, Blogger, TV Host, Influencer*

"I really loved reading this devotional. I love the businesswoman/entrepreneur twist that the writer incorporated. It felt like she wore her heart on her sleeve. It is great for both teens and women alike."

Nicole McCardy | *Pharmaceutical Scientist, Cosmetic Chemist, Sister of Adria Bee*

"*God and the GOAL Digger* is absolutely phenomenal. It's a devotional every woman should read. This is like a blueprint that will guide you along your journey. If you want to know what it means to be truly fulfilled, *God and the GOAL Digger* is the book for you."

Asline Blanc | *Accountant, Blogger/Writer, Editor, Trainer*

What's Coming:

Foreword		13
Introduction		16
Day 1	Doubt it? Do it Anyway.	23
Day 2	It's Okay to Not Know	29
Day 3	Ready. Set. God.	35
Day 4	Question Clichés	41
Day 5	Don't You Dare Slow Down, Love	47
Day 6	Know Your Crew – Friends or Nah?	59
Day 7	"I Pity the Hurt"	71
Day 8	It's Time for LISA	81
Day 9	L to the O-V-E Yourself	89
Day 10	Getting Back to Joy	95
Day 11	You are Enough	101
Day 12	No Purpose? No Problem	107
Day 13	Take the Road Less Trampled	113
Day 14	Let Them Help	119
Day 15	The Good, The Bad & The Green	127
Day 16	Stay Thankful	135
Day 17	Give it to God, Every Day	141
Day 18	A Woman's Worth	147
Day 19	Calm, Cool & Collaborate	153
Day 20	Check Your Circumstance	159

Day 21	Mirror Check	167
Day 22	Keep Forward	177
Day 23	You are the Person You've Been Waiting For	183
Day 24	Oprah Winfrey was Oprah Winfrey BEFORE becoming Oprah	189
Day 25	Make Your Own Adventure	195
Day 26	The Glass Half Full	203
Day 27	Hakuna Matata	209
Day 28	The Little Things are the Big Things	215
Day 29	My Favorite F Word	223
Day 30	Watch God Instead of People	229
Day 31	Trust God	235
Day 32	Watch God Again	241
Day 33	Know Your Triggers	249
Day 34	New Day. Who Dis? Taking Each Day as it Comes	255
Day 35	Think About Forever	261
Day 36	More Shorts and a Tee	273
Day 37	More Joy, Less Stress	279
Day 38	The Isolation of Moving On: The Hurt Habit	285
Day 39	Unplug	291
Day 40	God and The Professional	297

Foreword

I've lived a blessed life. Though I didn't grow up with material wealth, by 19, I'd traveled around the world, through Europe, and as far as Sri Lanka and Uganda representing The Bahamas as Regional Youth Caucus, Youth Ambassador to the Commonwealth. I've hosted a leading national TV show for the past 5 years. So many other wonderful stories exist in my journey, including my happy marriage, beautiful daughter and my social media marketing and PR company which has doubled in size in the last six months... but if I told you I had been happy through it all, I'd be lying.

For much of my blessed life, I've felt the weight of loneliness and the burden of being who I am. Have you ever been lonely? Or unhappy with who you are or how you looked, or even uncomfortable with some of the privileges you've enjoyed? We can do so much damage to ourselves in our loneliness, and I hope that this book can help you to stop, rethink and heal.

At the height of all I described to you above, the loneliness I felt led to me being in a relationship that was verbally abusive and damaged my self-esteem so strongly that I am still overcoming the limiting beliefs and feelings of unworthiness I put on myself at that time. I was able to come out of that relationship and get into one with my very best friend, but friendships have never been easy for me either.

The favor that is evidenced by all that I told you above made me stand out from my peers, and it made it extremely hard to keep friends. I remember feeling guilty about being blessed! I also remember nights of praying for friends that I could love and support and who would support me in return. I'm happy to say that though I can't boast of lifelong girlfriends, God has sent me my true few in recent years. I've also been able to use the power of our global community to find my tribe and the vibes are just right!

Whether your story is just like mine or far from it, we've all felt the burden of feeling like we didn't belong at one time or another. *God and the GOAL Digger* is a perfect guide to remind you that you may be lonely, but you are never alone because God's got you; He always keeps his own.

I love that Adria shares her experiences so openly in this book and I hope that by reading it, all of you unicorns who could never understand why you didn't fit in, will realize you were born to stand out. I hope that you know that there is a tribe of us here waiting for you to embrace your light and to thrive in it. The practical steps Adria provides in *God and the GOAL Digger* will bring you closer to God and help you to understand yourself, not as the world sees you, but as God does. It will also teach you how you can begin to use the internet to build a legacy and a community.

To my fellow Goal Diggers, whether you knew God before reading this book or will just discover Him in these pages, I am so happy you took the time to begin transforming your life. God has so many wonderful things in store for us. His word says that He wants to bless us with "more than we can ask, think, conceive or imagine according to the power that works within us." May this book empower you to unleash that power and may your cup overflow so that others can drink from it.

I can't wait to see all that you will be as you surrender to God, give up preconceived notions about what is possible and who you are, and open yourself up to all that God has called you to be, knowing that all things work together for the good.

Anastarcia Palacious
CEO & Confidence Coach

Foreword

Introduction

I've always wanted to be part of a girl group. But somehow, I would end up just like the leftovers of a Thanksgiving meal. You know, where the main courses like the turkey and mashed potatoes are a must, but you wouldn't really be bothered if there wasn't any corn or carrots? Yea, I'm the peas in the can... waiting to have a seat at the dinner table.

Okay ha-ha, that's being a bit dramatic; but in real terms, if I was in a group of five (5) and there were only four (4) concert tickets left.... You know how this ends: with me, Netflix and some popcorn and chocolate covered raisins (yummm) by myself, counted out, cast to the side.

There were times (I hate to admit), where these instances would leave me in a ball of tears. What was I doing wrong? Why I'm I always the afterthought? What can I do differently?

It was at those moments that I realized; *standing out was more 'me' than fitting in ever was.*

Welcome to the *God & the GOAL Digger* - A 40 Day Detox Devotional, where we will take the sometimes humorous yet personal journey of releasing society's goals and expectations, and instead focus (or re-focus) on learning how to seek

God's guidance in every aspect of our goals and our lives. Along our adventure, you will be introduced to *listening prayers* and *circle for success* sections that will help strengthen your connection with God and your faith for all the blessings to come.

Point of the Introduction: I brought up this story because there will be times in your goal-reaching journey where you feel at your highest, but also the *most alone*. This might be times where family and friends may not understand your vision; where you may no longer 'fit' in the groups, you're used to.

Though it can seem negative now, sometimes this transition is a sign of positive personal growth.

Keep Going.

Keep *Growing*.

In the words of one of my newly found quotes: Love, "you drown oceans" (Rupi Kaur). And what that means to me is - that you, my dear, are a *force* of nature. You *can* reach the impossible. What has started as remnants of an idea can turn into that multi-million empire you've been dreaming of. You are the X-factor of your success – impacting love and meaning along the way.

Whatever your new journey may be: motherhood, business, leisure, media, YouTube…, take the moments as they come, as part of a reevaluation of who you are and who and where you want to be.

Let's take the journey together.

For those who don't believe in God
I am not excluding you at all. I would love to learn more about what you stand for. I believe that truth can be found in a variety of places and that there are tips in here that can translate to women of every belief. As for why I include God in my writing, the explanation is simple: If we truly believe in something, our lives will reflect that, and as such, who God is and what He says we can do will be highlighted throughout my writing.

Know that this does NOT change my belief and love for you. I believe that you can achieve greatness and all that comes with it. Yet if you *still* decide not to read further on from this point, just know that you are truly beautiful and capable of anything – not despite but BECAUSE you are a strong woman! Know that God and I love you, and this starting point opens doors for continued conversation at whatever stage you are in your life.

A Note of Caution
This is NOT a book that aims to bash or berate other women, in fact, this book hopes to do the complete opposite. I hope that every woman (of every color, shape, size, and journey) who reads this will feel

confidently radiant in her own skin and will be able to empower others to do the same. I believe there is a specific confidence gap for women of faith in not only entrepreneurship but also, establishing ourselves in whatever venture we undertake – whatever that may look like.

As such, I aim to explore and address a few of these particular struggles (along with general struggles as a woman in today's society) in this detox devotional and ways we can eradicate them.

Your mind is your power.

Goal #1: Belief

Day 1

Doubt it? Do it Anyway.

*"The size of **your God** should determine the size of **your goal.**"*
Rick Warren

We're diving right in. The first reason you have not seen success in aspects of your life is simple: *You do not (really) believe in God and His ability in you.* Contrary to popular belief, belief is not a feeling – belief is a mindset and an *action* verb. Sometimes you have to proclaim your blessings, dreams and goals *before* there is any trace of them around you. Your belief in God and what He can do *directly* impacts the blessings God has for you.

The other reasons that may be hindering our life successes may not be as simple: we aren't praying with the right heart or request, we may not like God's response to those prayers, God may be telling us now is not the right time or… we don't want to do what we need to do to prepare for those blessings. Either way, belief in God, His power and what He can do through you is the first and *most important* step for seeing **unimaginable** results in your life.

> **#BibleCheck**
>
> *Matthew 9:29 says, "according to your faith, so it will be done to you."*

What do you think this verse is telling us? ...*The bigger our faith, the bigger our potential to experience God's blessings and wonder.*

We are the success or the failure of our own stories. Don't stunt the success God has waiting for you. God promises that He will take care of us and that we are to depend on Him. He is the Mighty God who parted the Red Sea, turned water into wine, and brought the dead back to life. Just I-M-A-G-I-N-E what He can do with your life - if you allow Him to.

Before going any further with this book, take this Word to heart: *What you believe determines your outcome.*

If you believe this book will be a waste of time – it *will* be. BUT if you believe when God says that with Him NOTHING is impossible, that He will move the mountains in your life if you only have the faith as small as a mustard seed – Then let's pull up our [stretchy] jeans and begin our journey together.

This book is divided into sections:

In addition to the "topic of the day," I intentionally implement intermittent Listening Prayers and Circle Proclamations. *Our goals go only as far as our belief.* Thus, as we go through these listening and circling times, trust that God will reveal Himself to you and the direction He has given you.

And, He will.

#Growth Check

Talking to God: We talk about prayer, but I would like to hit on the relational aspect of just communicating with God. Make a practice of just talking to God. Instead of talking to yourself when you're on the road against traffic, etc., talk to God about the everyday - start with the little things. Even if it sounds meaningless or like something extra to do, intentionally plan your day, including those everyday talks with God and watch your relationship grow.

Prayer Makes Things Happen

Dear Lord,

Thank You for this special time. A time to learn, grow, reflect, expose, heal and love. I put it all on the table. All my hurts, dreams, highs and lows – I give You the control to my life and my success. I

Doubt it? Do it Anyway.

believe when Your Word said in Ephesians 3:20 that You will grant me more than I can ever imagine, and I ask that You lead me in Your strength and direction. Life gets complicated, and there are times where societal influence may get the best of me. I pray that You will continue to take me out of the world in order to transform my thoughts and actions to be all who You have made me to be. I'm excited for this journey and to continue to grow in love and lessons with You. Please let not a single aspect of the life You created for me, pass me by. I love You and pray that my love only grows stronger as I am challenged to ask, learn, discuss and grow.

Your *loved* & *capable* daughter,

_____ (your name)

Amen

> *Now to him who is able to do immeasurably more than all we ask or imagine, according to his power that is at work within us.*
>
> Ephesians 3:20

> *"Blessed is she who has believed that the Lord would fulfill his promises to her!"*
>
> Luke 1:45

When God leads, you live.

Goal #2: Focus

Day 2

It's Okay to Not Know

"I see my path, but I don't know where it leads. Not knowing where I'm going is what inspires me to travel it."
Rosalia de Castro

I don't know what I'm doing with my life (yet); AND that's completely okay. But it wasn't always. I envied my siblings, friends, coworkers and those around me who always knew what they wanted to be when they grew up. Lawyer, Doctor, Actress, Chef – all eye-catching careers, but none of them ever stuck with me.

So what did this forever student do? I made my list and set out my goals as all the self-help books taught me. Here I laid my *What* (to get a job I liked), *Where* (somewhere on earth), *When* (ASAP), *Why* (to start a career) and *How* (working hard and keeping focused). And to be honest, my list looked semi-decent; I wasn't in love with how it turned out but was enthused that I had something to work towards.

Long-ish story short, what did I learn? Over the years my list adjusted and never really got to the point I wanted it to be. And it continued to be that way – *until it didn't*.

My mom and I were wrapping up another Listening Prayer (to be introduced *Day 7*) when one of the points God gave her was simple but life-changing: *It's not about where you are going, but **WHO** is leading you.*

Some may say, "Sure, we always say God is the leader of our life." But to get the realization that *we don't have to have the slightest direction to where our life is headed* is another level.

The world *repeatedly* tells us that we must have direction, we must find our passion, we HAVE TO figure out our purpose. BUT we've been going about it the wrong way. *It's not WWJD (What Would Jesus DO) but asking WHO we are in Jesus – the Son of the living, miracle-maker God.*

What am I saying? It honestly doesn't matter if you don't have the direction for your life. Now, if you know your passion, if you know your purpose – that is wonderful! But if you're like me and still don't have a clue – guess what – it is *still* wonderful! Why? Because you don't have to – God is the operator of your adventure. We ride rollercoasters with carefree excitement and enjoyment because we know *someone is operating the machinery*. How much more can we trust our own adventures if we know that God the Almighty, the All-knowing and the All-powerful is The Operator of our lives?

Love, *it is okay* not to know. In fact, sometimes it's even exciting. Whatever stage you are in, trust God to guide you. And if He doesn't reveal what He has for you just yet, don't spend a moment worrying – He is right there guiding you, every step of the way.

> **#GodandtheGoalDigger Check**
>
> **Click Click.** If you're starting a business or have a business online, having a good quality camera or phone with great camera quality is necessary. The market is increasingly visual, and the competition for visual space has also maximized. The good thing about this season of life is that you can find almost any tutorials online that can boost your camera/phone picture talent. A *Bonus* if you do invest in a good camera and begin learning those tricks is that you have now added a new potential skill that can make extra income if you so choose it.

Prayer Makes Things Happen

Dear Heavenly Father,

Thank You for who You are. Thank You that I don't have to have all the answers to be granted a

It's Okay Not to Know

fulfilled life. This may be one of the hardest things I will have to do. Letting You have all the control can sometimes make me feel lost and uncertain, but I continue to trust that You have the most excellent plan for me. How dare I even think that my plan could possibly be better than Yours! Yet Lord, I still need You and the encouragement along the way that You are with me and that You are working for me and within me. If I forget, please bring me back to the realization that You know me better than I will ever know myself and I can put my trust in You and Your leadership.

Your *loved* & *capable* daughter,

_____ (your name)

Amen

> *For who is God except the Lord? Who but our God is a solid rock? God is my strong fortress, and he makes my way perfect.*
>
> 2 Samuel 22:33

You want to be a
Game-Changer?
Ask the Life-Changer.

Goal #3: Truth

Day 3

Ready. Set. God.

"When you allow God to change your heart, He will also change your story."
Gift Gugu Mona

There are those that think that faith in God or even God Himself is a crutch. Which is completely ridiculous. Love, humans (like every other organism on this planet), have its imperfections. Yes, as humans, we can "use" God in a way that wasn't meant to be, but **that's on us**. If we walk with God *as He intended* – the whole trajectory of our lives changes. God wants to empower us on our journey – filling us with purpose and love.

You think "different" is what you see on the media? Often a high-profile citizen (such as celebrities) proclaims a .1% change in their life and it's exploited in every article as "This citizen defies the odds, doesn't care what anyone thinks…going against the norm." Not to negate the high-profile citizens that *are* doing amazing things, but my point is, most times, people end up doing much of the same – following the path of others. It's a shame that sometimes people fighting for real change every day get overlooked by those who decide to do something for a day and get all the publicity. **side tangent done**

Point: God is ready to work wonders in *you*. You want to be the proclaimed "different" that everyone is searching for these days? God is *the* most unconventional being around. When you put your trust in Him and go to Him each day for instruction – you may not even believe what He tells you. Some of what I thought to be the *most random* things that I felt led to do, has led me to some of the greatest moments of my life.

AND some of the most challenging. But the good news is that God is here to make you fully and truly who you were made to be. No, that doesn't mean you have to be the always church-going, open praying, dancing to gospel music person – it means that God is here for you – waiting to grow with you and help you get prepared for all the wonder He has in store for you. You just have to trust Him – daily.

> **#Growth Check**
>
> **Source of Inspirations:** Sometimes, church isn't enough. When I'm feeling lost or misguided, or just want to feel more connected, I find something online that teaches me something new about Christ and how to integrate Him in my life. Some of my (current) favorite pastors to find online is Pastor - Rick Warren, Steven Furtick, Michael Todd, Priscilla Shirer and Joel Osteen. Find someone online who you feel helps you grow in your walk of faith and challenge yourself through their discussions each day.

Prayer Makes Things Happen

Dear Almighty God,

Help me seek You, Lord. You. If I'm serious about my relational journey with You, then I want to know all about You. Reveal to me your characteristics when I read Your word and throughout my everyday life. I ask that You help me to continue to believe in You. Thank You for the unseen blessings that You will shower upon me when I least expect it.

Your *loved* & *capable* daughter,

_____ (your name)

Amen

Ready. Set. God.

I pray that God, the source of hope, will fill you completely with joy and peace because you trust in him. Then you will overflow with confident hope through the power of the Holy Spirit.

Romans 15:13

Get to know the most important person in your life - yourself.

Goal #4: Self-Awareness

Day 4

Question Clichés

"If you want to have a life that is worth living, a life that expresses your deepest feelings and emotions and cares and dreams, you have to fight for it."
Alice Walker

Clichés are meant to be challenged. We all hear the phrase, "If it won't matter five (5) years from now, don't let it bother you now."

Hmm…. Hmm…. Hmmm….

While I get the sentiment, the 'cliché instruction professionals' often forget to tell us is what to do in between. When we hear "don't let it bother you," we often think that means just push our feelings aside and not bring them up again. Allow me to rephrase this to say something even greater: **"Figure out why it matters, fully process it – in order to never let it bother you again."**

The difference between my rewording and the cliché phrase evokes learning and practical application. I can easily suppress things that have happened to me, but doing that will *not* solve the problem. In fact, those issues that you thought you "handled" tend to creep up and appear in different versions across your lifespan.

If you don't address your hurt – it can reappear in your life, stronger than before. In my lifetime, I've been left out of my share of opportunities, and the fact that I wasn't a part of them made me feel inadequate, not good enough, not qualified enough… the list goes on. And for a while, everything I looked at, whether it be a job application or even my relationships, those feelings of inadequacy followed me everywhere. *Sometimes one devastating let-down can cause you to rethink every aspect of your life.* Sure, what happened may not matter five (5) years from now, but if you don't explore and self-address what is going on inside of you in those moments, you stunt the growth that God is waiting to reveal to you.

Again, if it won't matter five (5) years from now, still work on figuring out why it bothers you **today,** process those emotions in order to heal and *then* work on moving forward.

> **#GodandtheGoalDigger Check**
>
> **Carry. Your. Contract.** Whether you are an Actress to Zipper Cutter (yes, it's a job), or doing personal work on the side from time to time, it is essential to have some documentation for the service you provide to entrust mutual protection. It can start out as simple as an email clearly defining what you are offering to the buyer, and that the buyer is interested in the services. My BFF (Best Finding Friend) Google, has thousands of contract templates ranging from different job sources. Put on your to-do list to find a sample contract that suits your needs today.

Prayer Makes Things Happen

Dear Father,

Thank You for giving me the ability to grow. I know there have been times where I struggle to trust and surrender to You. Lord, I ask You to bless each and every day as I go through this devotional.

Specifically, please open my eyes and heart to where I am hurt and help me to find the root of the problem so that I can begin to properly and fully heal. Even if it won't matter in a year –or even 10 years from now, please heal my heart so that I can

Question Clichés

move forward. Order my steps in prosperity and love.

Thank You for what You will do in this exciting yet challenging journey – I receive Your challenges for growth and blessing along the way. Thank You and Praise You!

Your *loved* & *capable* daughter,

_____ (your name)

Amen

> "Real contentment hinges on what's happening inside us, not around us."
>
> Charles Stanley

> *If our hearts condemn us, we know that God is greater than our hearts, and he knows everything.*
>
> 1 John 3:20

> *Peace I leave with you; My peace I give to you; not as the world gives do I give to you. Do not let your heart be troubled, nor let it be fearful.*
>
> John 14:27 (NASB)

You are worth the woman.

Goal #5: Identity

Day 5

Don't You Dare Slow Down, Love.

> "Women like you drown oceans."
> Rupi Kaur

Don't. You. Dare.

Let me introduce you to the *real* Proverbs 31 woman. A lot of Christian men reference the "Proverbs 31 woman" in terms of the ideal wife and marriage. But Love, if you look closely at the qualities listed within Proverbs 31, you realize that:

1. The Proverbs 31 woman was the very first *Goal Digger*: She in her own right worked extremely hard as an entrepreneur to see her business profit – she taught herself the deals of the trade to sustain herself and those around her (Proverbs 31:18;24)

2. Yes, she and her husband make a great team; but on her own, she is strong and dignified (Proverbs 31:25).

Don't You Dare Slow Down, Love.

3. She is a problem solver (Proverbs 31:21)

4. She loves generously helping those in need (Proverbs 31:20)

5. She is wise, intelligent and voices her opinion (Proverbs 31:26)

6. She is a *Phenomenal Leader* (Proverbs 31: 27-28)

7. So. Much. MORE!

Nowhere in this Proverbs 31 passage does it say the Proverbs 31 woman does this *for* her husband - stay with me...

Whether you are married, single, dating, complicating – You are God's masterpiece, first and foremost. Secondly, but equally as important – you are a *woman*. When God created you, He created YOU with an individual purpose. With the right tools, marriage is wonderful and extremely fulfilling, but don't let the idea of becoming his version of a Proverbs 31 woman neglect the unique purpose God has placed in you.

We (yes, me included) have a *bad habit* of dimming our shine to accommodate those who are not yet on our level.

"Oh, I'll meet them where they are, and then I'll get back to working on my personal growth," - says no one ever, but everyone does.

Don't you *dare* slow yourself down for the sake of letting others "catch up." Here are a couple of reasons why you shouldn't put a pause on your own personal growth:

1. It *is* possible to help others and continue to focus on your growth. If one comes in the way of your growth, then that is a sign that he, she or *it is not worth having*.

2. You are not in control. *God is*. He is working within you to bring out your purpose and though it may differ in timing with others – He has not forgotten you or them.

3. God is ready to do an *unimaginable* work in you! Don't miss out what He has for you to compensate for someone else.

4. Why slow down your potential for others behind you when there are those running alongside and ahead of you? Being the best you in Christ is not only the best for you, but also serves as a wealth of resources from those waiting to learn from you.

Don't You Dare Slow Down, Love.

5. The more you work on growing and loving yourself, *the more* you have to offer those around you. It really is a win-win after all.

This may seem like a harsh one, but it's one we need to hear. As women, often our natural go-to is to love, help and care for others first – which is an altruistic, beautiful thing. *But* how much can you give to others before your cup is empty? Knowing Whose you are and who you are as a woman before the wife, before the mother, before the other roles in your life are the greatest and most rewarding gifts you can give yourself – that lasts a lifetime.

To all the beautiful wives, mothers, daughters, entrepreneurs, stay-at-home moms, 9-5ers and all in between - I pray abundant joy, love and blessings overflow to you and yours. For the not-so-great times – including the breakups, fights, messes, and in sickness, etc.; the foundation you set *now* 1) in God and 2) in yourself as a holistic, gorgeous and capable woman, will dictate how you respond to every single challenge and blessing you encounter.

Don't you dare slow down, Love.

> **#Growth Check**
>
> **Know who you are.** We usually get a good sense of ourselves in our specific roles, but who are YOU apart from a wife, girlfriend, sister, and daughter? Who are you as a *Woman*? No matter what goes on through this lifetime, you are with yourself for the long run. Knowing who you are will serve as an anchor through all of your stages of life. Know that whatever stage you are in, you are entirely *whole* as a woman in Christ and of God. Embrace your womanhood today – take yourself on a mini date, write a *love letter* to yourself and look at it every time you forget the most treasured woman God has made in you.

Prayer Makes Things Happen

Dear Lord,

Thank You for the strength and beauty You have made in women. We live in a society where sometimes our attributes are overlooked or only spoken about in relation to having a partner. Partner or not, I pray that You will reveal to me what all a woman is – and who I am as a woman in Christ. Help me to hold fast to this through all stages of life, being able to

Don't You Dare Slow Down, Love.

wholeheartedly know and love the woman You created me to be. Help this be the first step into fulfilling all the other roles that come into my life. Help me to keep You first, but also that I keep a sense of what it means to be a woman, in Christ and within myself. You say You have made me in awe and wonder, please give me Your eyes to see how special I am to You and those around me.

Your *loved* & *capable* daughter,

_____ (your name)

Amen

[13] She selects wool and flax and works with eager hands. [14] She is like the merchant ships, bringing her food from afar. [15] She gets up while it is still night; she provides food for her family and portions for her female servants. [16] She considers a field and buys it; out of her earnings she plants a vineyard. [17] She sets about her work vigorously; her arms are strong for her tasks. [18] She sees that her trading is profitable, and her lamp does not go out at night. [19] In her hand she holds the distaff and grasps the spindle with her fingers. [20] She opens her arms to the poor and extends her hands to the needy. [21] When it snows, she has no fear for her household; for all of them are clothed in scarlet. [22] She makes coverings for her bed; she is clothed in fine linen and purple. [23] Her

husband is respected at the city gate, where he takes his seat among the elders of the land. [24] *She makes linen garments and sells them, and supplies the merchants with sashes.* [25] *She is clothed with strength and dignity; she can laugh at the days to come.* [26] *She speaks with wisdom, and faithful instruction is on her tongue.* [27] *She watches over the affairs of her household and does not eat the bread of idleness.* [28] *Her children arise and call her blessed; her husband also, and he praises her:* [29] *"Many women do noble things, but you surpass them all."* [30] *Charm is deceptive, and beauty is fleeting; but a woman who fears the Lord is to be praised.* [31] *Honor her for all that her hands have done, and let her works bring her praise at the city gate.*

Proverbs 31: 13-31

Circle for Success

Congratulations! You've made it to Day 5, and I am so proud of you! I pray that even now that God begins to reveal to you His secrets for the blessings and tasks of your life.

You've now entered the part of the book where you will proclaim your blessings. One of my theme verses from The Bible: "*Now to him who is able to do above and beyond all that we ask or think according to the power that works in us*

Don't You Dare Slow Down, Love.

(Ephesians 3:20 CSB)" is real! He can do above and beyond our wildest dreams! It may not be in the way we imagined it – but it will be even better if you let God lead!

This next step, every 5 days, we will call *Circle for Success*. Why? Because this is your *check-in-point*, Miss Goal Digger. You will be addressing your goals in every aspect of your life by physically circling and praying through them.

Thank you, Mark Batterson, for giving us the innovative book, *The Circle Maker* (Batterson, 2011) and *Draw the Circle* (Batterson, 2012) and the inspiration for our Circle for Success proclamations.

Love, as much as you must believe in your goals and dreams, the more profound belief should be in the God, who provides them!

We often look to God as an afterthought, rather than our go-to/main provider. In this Circle for Success journey, you will start circling your dreams and goals prayerfully – and with intention. God's power is limitless, and as such, we should have no doubt about His ability to bring all that He has for us, to fruition.

Circle for success: *The Core*

The first day add your core to the circle. Your core is whoever or whatever you want to keep the closest. For example, my core consists of my loved ones: such as my family, close friends, etc.

For this coming week, *come back to this section* and prayerfully go through your list with confidence and humility before God – and watch God work in, through and for you.

Think about who and what you want in your *core* and place it in the circle below:

The Core

Don't You Dare Slow Down, Love.

he true few starts with the few true.

Goal #6: Friendship

Day 6

Know Your Crew – Friends or Nah?

"Find a group of people who challenge and inspire you; spend a lot of time with them, and it will change your life."
<u>Amy Poehler</u>

While God is the *core* of our success, our support system is the *cornerstone*. Before we can get on our independent, goal-reaching livelihood, it's important to know and understand some of the different types of friends we encounter throughout our lives, and how emotionally invested, we can comfortably become. In honor of my **love** for MOVIES, let's do this #FilmStyle:

The Rom-Coms

Romantic Comedies (commonly known as Rom-Coms) are the light-hearted films that amuse us, make us laugh and make us feel good inside. The movie has some drama but doesn't get deep enough for our feelings to linger. And once the movie is over, we file it away in our romantic comedy ratings and wait for the next Rom-Com blockbuster. The Rom-Com is better known as the *seasonal friend*. Like romantic comedies, you enjoy the friend's company while it lasts: you laugh with them, cry with them, but at some point, they move on, or you've moved on from that point in your life.

Like Rom-Coms, not all seasonal friends are bad, in fact, as we continue to change and find ourselves, we sometimes just outgrow the company we were used to having. Sometimes we even go back and binge-watch our favorite Rom-Coms again, but eventually, Love, we absorb our nostalgic fix and get back to other genres... get ready for the next movie.

The Pre-views

Traditionally, previews for movies only show up when a movie is coming soon. You get a little bit of what the film is going to be like, but after the movie is out in theaters, the previews for those movies also cease. Welcome the *convenient friend*. The difference between a Rom-Com and the Pre-views is that the Pre-views tend to focus more on proximity than seasons. This is the type of friend that shows up when you are back in town, but you hear nothing from when you go back to college or work. If you're around them, then great, you can be friends, but once you leave within certain proximity: out of sight... out of... you know the rest. Anything more would be, well.... inconvenient. Like Rom-Coms, the Previews are not necessarily negative but can be misleading if you were planning to watch the whole film.

The Box Office

To a movie producer, the Box Office gross is extremely important. If the movie generates exceeding funds, the producer is ecstatic and can't wait to do more parts of the same film story. But if the Box Office plummets, chances are, the movie producer is out looking for the next big hit. Welcome the *gimme,* AKA the *give-me friend.* This type of friend only looks for what you can give to them. *They emotionally drain you.* You may notice that they'll show up when you recently received a big promotion or when things are just going well for you. They want to know all about your life and are telling you that they will be there for you whenever you need them. They make you feel like a priority. But this is also the same friend that when you express any level of doubt or concern about your life, they conveniently remove themselves out of the equation. Because to them, the Box Office (i.e., friendship) is only as good as the money it makes (i.e., the benefits received in the relationship). Be careful if you have this type of friend in your life. While it's a blessing to give and help others, remember that the essence of "friend" is meant for a reciprocating relationship.

The Re-boots

You know the ones. These are the movies that we already know the story all too well; they may hire new actors, but the bulk of the plot remains the same. There is some creative license taken, but for the most part, the movie is producing existing pretenses. You already know how the plot will progress, yet you still want to see what aspects were kept and what changes were made and if they were for the better or worse. Welcome the *let-me-down friend*. You already know this type of friend's character, but you keep forgiving and hoping that the "end result" will change. This is my kryptonite. I've seen 'friends' who do nothing for me but time and time again I forgive and make myself believe that they have changed. And time and time again I have re-opened the same wounds, just to be cut deeper. My lovely Goal Diggers, I am not saying that people are unchangeable, but I am saying that if you have a friend that only seems to tweak minor, surface-level appearances to make you believe that they have changed, more likely than not, they haven't, and it's time to exit the theater.

And finally...

The Classics

We all have our favorite movies that we can watch anytime and still get that warm feeling inside: the movies that will never get old; the movies that remind us of better times. Though as we get older, the meaning of these movies may alter and shift... but the love remains constant. The classic movies stay with us and become a part of our living fabric. We attach these movies to special moments of our lives, and no matter how different each classic is from the other, they all play a part in how we view ourselves and in who we are. As you could have guessed, welcome the *lasting friend*. This is a friend that you can talk to every day or every year, and you can just pick up where you left off. You know this friend cares for you and will be there no matter what. And even though your "friendship" may look slightly different over the years, you know that this is someone you can count on. All you have to do is pick up the phone, and they will be right there to answer. These friends are special treasures – CHERISH THEM!

A Special Note

We truly thank God for the Classics in our lives, but we should also thank Him for all the other types of friends. You see, ALL categories of friends have helped us learn and grow so that when a rare Classic comes into our lives, we are able to recognize it and treat them as they deserve – with respect, truth, and love. You don't have to give up the other types of friends; in fact, they can all carry out a *different* purpose. But, it is imperative to know and assess what kind of friends you have so that you can put up the necessary boundaries to promote healthy existing friendships – and make way for new ones.

#GodandtheGoalDigger Check

Write your own personal list of each of the #FilmStyle friend above and sort out where you think each of your friends should be. After listing, take the time to ask God for His opinion on each type of friend and how to wholesomely invest (or not invest), in each one of their lives:

 ꞏ **Rom-Com** (Seasonal Friends)

- **Pre-views** [Convenient Friends]

- **Box Office** [Give-Me Friends]

- **Re-boots** [Let-Me-Down Friends]

Know Your Crew – Friends or Nah?

> ♪ **Classics** [Lasting Friends]

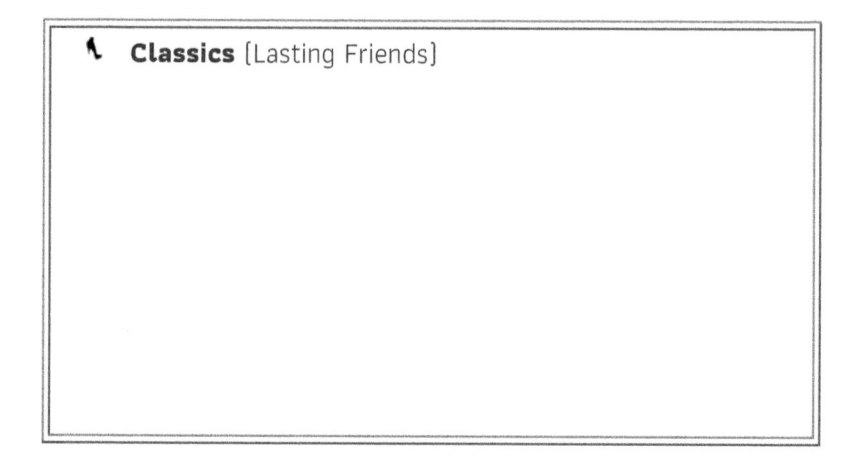

Prayer Makes Things Happen

Lord,

Friendship is one of the greatest treasures You placed here for us on this earth. And yet some of our deepest hurts come from friendships gone wrong or friendships lack thereof. Either way, Lord, I ask that You surround me with people *You* have for my life.

Surround me with people of positivity, motivation, truth and love. And where there is lacking, I ask that You fill me with trust, joy and contentment in You, each step of the way. I pray that You bless me with the discernment of choosing friends wisely – in a way that is directed and pleasing in Your eyes. Thank You for the opportunity to grow, and please continue to be with me on this adventure.

Your *loved* & *capable* daughter,

_____ (your name)

Amen

"There is nothing on this earth more to be prized than true friendship."

Thomas Aquinas

One who has unreliable friends soon comes to ruin, but there is a friend who sticks closer than a brother.

Proverbs 18:24

Build a habit worth having.

Goal #7: The Road to Healing

Day 7

"I Pity the Hurt"

"To heal your wound, you need to stop touching it."
Dwight Moody

Sticks and stones may break my bones, but words *definitely* hurt me. The hurt process goes more or less like this: Offender hurts you (emotionally/verbally) → you feel devastated → you try to forget it/move on → emotional trigger → more feelings of pain and devastation → wanting to move on, but so used to holding the emotional grudge.

The human brain is a habit-forming machine. So, while you were hurt, the brain triggered the feelings of distress, loss, and pain associated with your hurt. As you continued to be offended, your mind formulated a routine of learned responses towards the hurt situation. Unsurprisingly, it will take the same type of process to get back to healing. And yes, it takes a bit of time. We cannot expect months of feeling hurt and desolation to turn into a day of full joy and forgiveness. Like the routine you developed during your hurt stage, it's the same process you will take (unless God supernaturally resolves it in an instant) to forgive and move on gracefully.

While we're sitting down hurt, maybe eating our feelings in ice cream (my favorite cookies and cream) or working out (...again mmm ice cream!), the offender is often RELAXING. The said person is RESTING comfortably – without a care in the world – and has more than likely – moved on – living their best life: *Which means that the only one left hurting is you*. If your goal of hurt was to receive solace, that ship quickly sailed. People can feel guilty for a short period, but after that, the act of normalcy takes place, and you are left alone again having to deal. I'm NOT saying refuse to hurt; we all need to address and somewhat dwell-in all the hurt aspects. But Love, "**You are worth so much more than another's time stamp.**" Let's now choose to take a step back, address that hurt, and actively seek steps towards being healed.

From Hurt to Heal

- Be Thankful
- Find the Good in the person who has hurt you
- Take a step back –pause– then come back with a more controlled sense of the situation.

- Pretend that you are the person who has hurt you. Write an apology letter from them to you – expressing all you wish they would say.

- Confront them about how you feel if this is appropriate and reasonable. (This step is optional as there may be extenuating circumstances making it impossible.)

If people want to be in your life genuinely, they'll listen and respond accordingly. If not, then it may be time to **let them go**.

#GodandtheGoalDigger Check

Take a step back and look at your goals. Who or what are they for? If they aren't for what's important to you and your journey with God, re-evaluate and adjust the "Why" for your goals. It may seem small now but finding out what really drives your passion is the difference between a fling of success and lasting impact.

Prayer Makes Things Happen

Dear Lord,

Please intervene with my habit of hurt. Help me first to *want* to feel better and then show me how

"I Pity the Hurt"

to do so. But I don't just want to feel better – I want to *heal*. Please provide me with Your healing instruction day by day so that I can be stronger in You and to administer what You have for me to do. Thank You for Your kindness and mercy. And even though I may not be able to see myself out of this situation, please lend me Your eyes and Your heart so that I can push through.

Your *loved* & *capable* daughter,

_____ (your name)

Amen

> *Get rid of all bitterness, passion, and anger. No more shouting or insults, no more hateful feelings of any sort. Instead, be kind and tender-hearted to one another, and forgive one another, as God has forgiven you through Christ.*
>
> **Ephesians 4:31-32** (GNT)

Introducing: The Listening Prayer

Simple, Significant and So Worth It!

During the remainder of the 40 days, our action steps will include *listening prayer*.

In a world of "*busy*," taking even the slightest amount of time, apart from daily life, can seem painstakingly tasking. But experientially, listening prayers is the one single thing I would never regret. We say we want success, but often forget our most successful resource: becoming in tune with what God has for you. As you take 5-8 minutes of uninterrupted time with Christ, I (prayerfully) guarantee that you will gain a sense of direction of your present and future (Amen).

Listening How-to(s):

1. Find a quiet spot for your listening session (for me, it's in bed when I get up).

2. Block your thoughts relating to the daily to do's etc. by following the pattern of the Listening Prayer below.

3. Open your mind and spirit so that you can receive God's "words" for you.

4. Wait and Listen freely.

"I Pity the Hurt"

5. Write all your thoughts, songs, visions, etc. during this time-period down.

***Note: Sometimes you may not hear/see/feel anything, other times you may be overloaded with information. Either way, continue the time with Him and watch your growth and development.

Learning to Listen: The Prayer

(Adapted from Mary Geegh's *God Guides*) (Geegh, 2014)

Almighty Father, I receive James 1:5 and come to You in the beloved name of Jesus Christ, seeking wisdom, direction, and guidance for _____.

In Jesus' name and in agreement with Luke 10:19 & 20 and Matthew 28:18, I take total authority over Satan and his demons. I command that they will become blind, deaf, and dumb to my intentional listening and prayers, and be completely removed from my presence. I also place my own thoughts and desires under Jesus' authority and command that my thoughts will obey Christ as commanded in 2 Corinthians 10:5. Please, Lord, I ask that only your Holy Spirit will speak to me as I await Your wisdom, direction, and insights for _____. Whatever You reveal and direct me to venture, I will quickly obey. Amen.

[Please note: God will never go against His Word.]

Set your timer & Pause for your 3-10 minutes moment of intentional listening and being with Him

Guidance in the Silence

Even if it doesn't make sense right now, write down what you saw, heard, felt – everything, below:

_____
_____
_____
_____
_____
_____
_____
_____
_____
_____

"I Pity the Hurt"

***Sometimes you may not fully understand what you hear/see during these times, but as you go along, what you thought was random may end up connecting and becoming a constant thread rather than a scattered appearance. Ask God for guidance and confirmation – He will show it to you.

Listening Prayer Scripture References

If any of you lacks wisdom, you should ask God, who gives generously to all without finding fault, and it will be given to you.

James 1:5

I have given you authority to trample on snakes and scorpions and to overcome all the power of the enemy; **nothing** *will harm you.[20] However, do not rejoice that the spirits submit to you, but rejoice that your names are written in heaven."*

Luke 10:19-20

Then Jesus came to them and said, "All authority in heaven and on earth has been given to me.

Matthew 28:18

We demolish arguments and every pretension that sets itself up against the knowledge of God, and we take captive every thought to make it obedient to Christ.

2 Corinthians 10:5

Vulnerability is strength.

Goal #8: Vulnerability

Day 8

It's Time for LISA

"Vulnerability is the birthplace of connection and the path to the feeling of worthiness. If it doesn't feel vulnerable, the sharing is probably not constructive."
Brene Brown

L-I-S-A: Letting In Someone Again. God wants you to be surrounded by growth, trust, and love. Sometimes this means allowing God to remove people from your life, and trusting Him to embrace those He brings in. You may think to yourself, "Why is *'relationship'* a recurring theme in a *God and The GOAL Digger* Devotional book?" The answer is simple: *Your entrepreneurial venture only grows as much as you grow.*

There are Three (3) things that lead you to thrive in this Goal Digger City:

1. God
2. Intentional, Personal Growth
3. Your circle of support.

Gaining the wisdom and discernment of who to let into your life (and who to allow to exit) is a crucial part of becoming your best self in this beloved sisterhood.

1. God

It took me (and is still taking me) a while to keep God at the forefront. Honestly (*sorry, Lord*), I felt like the "breadth" that I had to get done in a day was more urgent than taking out, even five minutes, with God. Some days it literally seemed like a waste of time (*again, so sorry!*). Love, I could never be more wrong.

God is the *Accelerator*. When you think, "I can solely control myself without God's help and guidance," you have less control than before. Don't confuse this with taking the initiative/courage – I'm specifically targeting when we no longer see God as our guide and leader.

When I was in the search for jobs and working on my entrepreneurship journey, there were times I decided to take everything into my own hands. I selected not to seek His counsel, and instead, I chose to do what I thought was going to be a sure fit. It's so funny now: I could just see God laughing at my feeble attempts! Nothing quite worked out even near to its full potential, UNTIL I gave it back to God.

The moment I gave full control back to God is the moment I started seeing the overflow of His blessings, guidance and love.

> **#Point:** To my Take-Over-The-World-ers, God is *never* a hindrance to your success. It may not be entirely the vision you set for yourself, but if God is in it, rest assured that it will be nothing short of amazing!

2. **Intentional, Personal Growth**

They say to grow you have to *want* to. Nevertheless, sometimes in life, staying the same is the most comfortable and convenient way of living. Yes, some growth can happen naturally (e.g. through situations you have been placed in); but the most significant growth often comes from *making the decision* to read, write, explore – look for things that can help reshape your mindset and put you on the accelerated track for growth. Giving control of your life to God is also a sign of personal growth.

3. **Your circle of support**

Oddly enough, your circle of support often comes during your time of self-exploration, growth and dedication to God. But if it doesn't, trust that God is working on it for you. I've gone from a dry period of friendships to watching new or re-born friendships blossom. Don't be afraid to go out and try something new. Who knows, you might meet some friends along the way.

My all-capable Goal Diggers, I pray that you will be vulnerable enough to let God direct your life – revealing to you all the wonders He has in store.

Hint: You may have to: Give it (control) back to Him each day.

> **#Growth Check**
>
> In your listening prayers, **ask God to reveal the aspects that should be released to Him** – He will show you from there.

Prayer Makes Things Happen

Lord,

We thank You for the people we have chosen and the people You have placed to be in our life. We know that some are here for life, and others may be here for learned lessons – some may be here for both. We ask that You bless not the quantity of friends but the quality of the friendships we make now and moving forward in our journey. Thank You for giving us the gift of love in friendship, and please serve as a guide for our relationships –

giving us the wisdom, discernment and vulnerability when seen fit.

Your *loved* & *capable* daughter,

_____ (your name)

Amen

> *Of course, my friends, I really do not think that I have already won it; the one thing I do, however, is to forget what is behind me and do my best to reach what is ahead. So I run straight toward the goal in order to win the prize, which is God's call through Christ Jesus to the life above.*
>
> **Philippians 3:13-14** (GNT)

The best gift you can give to the world is loving yourself.

Goal #9: You

Day 9

L to the O-V-E Yourself

*"Love yourself first and everything else falls into line. You really have to love yourself to get **anything** done in this world."*
Lucille Ball

Life can only extend to the furthest love you set for yourself. Loving yourself helps you, to not only love God more but others and life around you. The term 'loving yourself' can get a bit twisted when we only refer to our spending habits and self-indulgence(s). Beautifuls, (if it's not a word, it is now), here is a quick L-O-V-E guide whenever you find yourself forgetting:

L: Learn. Listen. Love.

- *Learn* new things that help define who you are.
- *Listen* for what inspires you, rather than what drains you.
- *Love* yourself the way God meant you to – unconditionally.

O: Be Original

What cracks me up in society is that we have a world of 'Stand-Out Fanatics' who end up doing the *same thing* everyone else does. Talk with God and find out your personal perspective on life and go from there.

V: Vulnerability

Be real with yourself, just like when no one's watching. Let God know all of your negative, positive, deepest feelings, not just how you are 'supposed' to feel.

E: [NO] Excuses

This life here can't be redone. The things you want to do – intentionally set your goals to get there – whether that be learning a new skill or continuing to practice your dream. Remember: *With God, nothing is impossible.*

#GodandtheGoalDigger Check

Set up your daily planner, with an intentional section set for yourself – whether that means intentionally scheduling rest time, doing something you like or investing in a new skill. Let that intentional time be one of purpose and direction. And of course, bring fun along the way ☺.

Prayer Makes Things Happen

Heavenly Father,

Help me to learn how to love myself truly. Sometimes I seek love in material things, but Lord, also help me to love myself in ways that *last*. Show me authentic ways to love myself that help me to grow, love and *thrive*.

Your *loved* & *capable* daughter,

_____ (your name)

Amen

"Nothing is impossible. The word itself says 'I'm possible'!"

Audrey Hepburn

To acquire wisdom is to love oneself; people who cherish understanding will prosper.

Proverbs 19:8

Happiness relies on circumstance; get you some joy.

Goal #10: Joy

Day 10

Getting Back to Joy

"If you carry joy in your heart, you can heal any moment."
Carlos Santana

There is this notion that we have to always get back to "happy." When in reality, Life. Sometimes. Just. Happens. In life, there is loss, pain, struggle, and hurt, and there are times where we have to feel through those moments so we can heal and grow. I find that the happiness that people portray often comes with a touch of superficiality. Yes, we all smile for the camera, but what happens when the camera and phones are put away? Can we honestly say we are happy with who we are and what we do?

Enter Joy.

God never promised us forever happiness on earth. In fact, when you search "Bible verses about happiness," chances are you see more verses on joy and gladness. The thought of happiness has been trivialized to a matter of circumstance rather than an inner glow that's impossible to hide. Joy tells us that, yes, there is sadness – and that's okay, but that these emotions are some of the components that make joy possible.

Love, let's *breathe* together. It is *completely* okay not to be happy all the time – actually, life guarantees that there will be some tough moments to get through. Luckily for us, God promises that joy can remain in our hearts through trusting His love and His plan for us that no one can take away.

> **#Growth Check**
>
> **Mirror Mirror.** Sometimes without reflection, we can miss what God has been saying to us all along. Take a minute or two and just reflect on your growth thus far and write down the steps that helped you get there. On the side of those steps, also write an encouraging word or note during those victory days. And during the tough times, re-read these steps and encouragements and continue to add additional ones to keep moving forward.

Prayer Makes Things Happen

Dear Heavenly Father,

Thank You that I don't have to force happiness. Help me to understand that sometimes, pain is the greatest teacher. And if not for those moments of trials and struggle, I would never get to the fulfilled life You've promised me. In these hard times, I also ask that You help me find joy – joy in knowing that this time is just a season and will be rewarded a hundredfold as I continue to walk with You. Help me to turn pain into progress and purpose so that I won't even recognize my (spiritual) self the next time I look in the mirror.

Your *loved* & *capable* daughter,

_____ (your name)

Amen

> *There is a time for everything, and a season for every activity under the heavens…a time to tear down and a time to build, a time to weep and a time to laugh, a time to mourn and a time to dance.*
>
> Ecclesiastes 3: 1; 3b-4

Circle for Success: *Health*

A lot of times, we take this step for granted. If we are already "healthy" sometimes we forget to cover our health in prayer. There is also always something that we can improve about our life health choices: including eating habits and diet.

Getting Back to Joy

For this coming week, *come back to this section* and prayerfully go through your list with confidence and humility before God – and watch God work in, through and for you.

List some of your *health* goals in the circle provided below:

Health

God makes NOTHING half-way.
"You complete, Boo"

Goal #11: Whole

Day 11

You are Enough

"A woman without a man is like a fish without a bicycle."
Gloria Steinem

Let's do some math. We've heard some say that Half (1/2) You + Half (1/2) Him = One (1). NOPE. You are COMPLETE without a significant other. Partner or no partner, God is the ultimate filler of our lives. If we continue to believe that somewhere our "other half" is out there waiting to fulfill all our needs, we will *never* be satisfied. If you are looking for a partner, search for a "whole" (a significant other that is complete in God), rather than a half. This positive action results in raising the bar to a higher standard – not only for your potential mate in life – but for yourself – to be a "whole" as you progress in life. So mate or no mate, Your value is whole in Christ. Just imagine all you can do as a "Whole!" Grow and Own it, *Love*.

New Equation: One (1) Whole You + God = One (1) and done (complete in Him)!

> **#Growth Check**
>
> **Take God out of the box.** On one of your devotional days, switch things up a bit, and take God on a date. My JAM (Jesus and Me) dates usually involve some food and (or) a beach. Our God is not just present and available for monotonous interventions; it was He who made this exciting, vast, adventurous world. And His affiliation with us is ideally one of the most diverse relationships known to man — so let's try to keep it that way: keep it interesting!

Prayer Makes Things Happen

Dear Lord,

Remind me that I am *enough* in You. Thank You for placing everything I need to accomplish my purpose in this world already inside of me. Please stand with me and guide me to maximize the gifts You have given me to fulfill Your and my purpose. Thank You for Your ever-lasting, ever-knowing & ever-forgiving love.

Your *loved* & *capable* daughter,

_____ (your name)

Amen

And to know the love of Christ which surpasses knowledge that you may be filled up to all the fullness of God.

Ephesians 3:19

But whoever is united with the Lord is one with him in spirit.

1 Corinthians 6:17

Faith is taking the risk to fall so that you can fly.

Goal #12: Faith

Day 12

No Purpose? No Problem.

"You may not be like everyone else, but that's okay. Be who God made you to be."
Victoria Osteen

Have we met yet? My name is Adria: I'm a Giver and a devoted Lemon-water drinker (It's just so gooood!). I am also known as a graduate of a Master's in Communication – aka, until very recently, I had no official job. The problem I believed I had was that I was an admirer of many things, but passionate about none. Or so I thought.

I yearned to be one of those individuals who just knew what their passion was. My sisters loved science; my brother loved history. And me, well I just fell into things. My Bachelor's in Psychology was achieved, strongly due to the fact that I took AP (Advanced Placement) Psychology in high school rather than AP English, My Master's in Communication resulted because, apparently, "no one can survive on only a Psychology Bachelor's." Did I enjoy these majors? Of course! But were they my passions? Still working on that answer...

If I knew just twenty percent (20%) of what my purpose in life was, I would be driving FULL force towards it. Once we Goal Diggers set our mind on something – that's it!

Nevertheless, God gives us what we need to depend on Him. If we only needed to know twenty percent (20%) of what our purpose in life was, He may give us ten percent (10%) so that the other ten percent (10%), relies on having faith in Him. If you had all the answers you needed, *there would be no reason for God*. When we turn our reliance on ourselves solely, we can miss all the wonders God has tucked away for us. **Never let determination confuse your dedication to God's glory.** Darling, even in the core of confusion, God has an incredible, unimaginable adventure planned for you *(and me)*. In Jesus Name!

> **#GodandtheGoalDigger Check**
>
> **M-E-D-I-A.** Social media has granted us the flexibility and opportunity like never before. Whatever your idea is: from documenting Mom-hood to your 9 to 5 to sharing your creation – Create your "space" that is entirely yours. A starting tip is to find social media profiles that you enjoy and like as inspiration for what you can work towards. If you are *already* an expert in media, look for phone editing apps (my personal fave is Snapseed), so you can create even more engaging and higher quality content. More media tips to come in this section as we go along.

Prayer Makes Things Happen

Father,

Thank You for giving me a purpose. Even when I may not know what it entails, thank You for placing it in me. You know my purpose even before I was in my mom's womb. Please reveal hints along my journey for me to walk in that purpose. Comfort me in the times where I question what my purpose it, but above all – continue to help me walk in You through it all.

No Purpose? No Problem.

Your *loved* & *capable* daughter,

_____ (your name)

Amen

> *Being confident of this, that he who began a good work in you will carry it on to completion until the day of Christ Jesus.*
>
> **Philippians 1:6**

Seasons of true growth are often the most lonely.

Goal #13: Standing Alone

Day 13

Take the Road Less Trampled

"The truth is that entrepreneurship is more like a roller coaster ride than a cruise."
Vivek Wadhwa

I always wanted to go into business with my closest friends. I think my friends are some of the most driven, innovative, and go-getting people of all-time – OF COURSE, I would want to go into business with them. But that wasn't the plan God had for me (at least not at this moment). Instead, He isolated me from friends so I could work on other projects.

God places trials in your life for a reason. I grew up having lots of friends, but it was at a time where I felt the most alone that God used me to expand my entrepreneurial thinking. I pulled up my [cute but comfy stretchy] jeans yet again and got to learning and working. I began writing for people, from company summaries to social media consulting. I picked up and started working on photography. I refused to let hearing resounding "No's" from potential employers and not being chosen by partners and their businesses, hinder my personal growth.

You can do the same. You cannot let the absence of company (and people) deter you from your goals. What God put in you, He is one hundred percent (100%) capable of pulling out of you and carrying you through all the necessary steps to accomplish your purpose. If He thinks you need someone beside you to help you with these goals, by all means, He will provide the right person! But until then, trust in His prosperous plan, with His *perfect timing.*

If the only thing you were waiting on was for someone to tell you that you can do it, hear me now (and the millions of people you don't even know as yet): *You are made in the image of God. You are a child of the living God who can move oceans and valleys in the blink of an eye!* Just imagine what He can prepare you to do. *You most definitely* are capable of whatever venture you set, and with God's guidance, you will do it phenomenally!

> **#Growth Check**
>
> **Add the word "Passion" to your Day 5 Core Circle for Success.** Choose two things that you most enjoy and circle them each day – first thing when you get up. Claim your goals and watch where God takes you.

Prayer Makes Things Happen

Dear Heavenly Father,

I know sometimes I will stand alone from worldly influences. Thank You for never leaving my side. Help me remember that even alone You are with me. I pray for the day that I truly believe that You are the ingredient to my success here on earth and in heaven.

If an idea seems crazy or just a little bit nerve-wracking, please remind me that with You, I can do anything. And that I do not always need the support or approval of others to start something I believe in. But I do ask for Your wisdom during this venture. Please reveal to me if _____ is something You want me to do and if it isn't, please take the opportunity away. I put my business/this decision in Your control. Thank You.

Take the Road Less Trampled

Your *loved* & *capable* daughter,

_____ (your name)

Amen

"I took the one less traveled by, and that has made all the difference."

Robert Frost

Forget the former things; do not dwell on the past.

Isaiah 43:18

Have I not commanded you? Be strong and courageous. Do not be afraid; do not be discouraged, for the Lord your God will be with you wherever you go.

Joshua 1:9

Support = Success

Goal #14: Accepting Help

Day 14

Let Them Help

"For there is no friend like a sister in calm or stormy weather; To cheer one on the tedious way, to fetch one if one goes astray, to lift one if one totters down, to strengthen whilst one stands."
Christina Rossetti

Even proclaimed "sole ventures" consist of a team helping them along the way. You always hear that you are who your friends are and that your surroundings make up your identity. Similarly, there is often a crew (whether personal or public figures) who help guide you on the road to success. Rather than looking at receiving help as a weakness, seek it as a *privilege*. Life is a whirlwind of stories and bits and pieces coming together to make up this adventure we call life. Today's task is for you to allow help from others, into your life. Let others be even just a small part of your journey. You'll find that your story can become even richer, and prayerfully, new opportunities will start knocking.

#BibleCheck

Proverbs 15:22 says, *"Plans fail for lack of counsel, but with many advisers they succeed."*

#GodandtheGoalDigger Check

As of when this book was published, Instagram is one of the highest (if not the highest) leading tool for getting your product or vision out there. The most recent nine pictures (9 pic grid) on Instagram are what people will see when they stumble on your profile. Make sure each 9-pic segment portrays the "feel" of your page and how you want it to be perceived. *Planoly* is a great app/website tool that allows you to upload and test out your picture layout before posting on Instagram. There is a free sign up for you to plan your posts, and if you want to make further use of this tool (allowing unlimited uploads, for example), you can upgrade to a low charge, alternative monthly plan.

Prayer Makes Things Happen

Lord,

I know I think I can figure out everything on my own. But if that were the case, life would've been sorted out by now. Thank You for being with me even when I don't act like I need You. The truth is, I do – more than I can ever know.

I also know that there will be times where I may need help from others. Please help me to be vulnerable enough to receive this help and willing enough to help others out when needed. I ask for Your continued blessings and discernment for me and those around me – that we may honor and serve You in all that we do.

Your *loved* & *capable* daughter,

_____ (your name)

Amen

> *"When you receive God's love and encouragement, it will empower you to do more than you ever thought possible."*
>
> Victoria Osteen
>
> *Each of us should please our neighbors for their good, to build them up.*
>
> Romans 15:2

Let Them Help

Learning to Listen: The Prayer

(Adapted from Mary Geegh's *God Guides*) (Geegh, 2014)

Almighty Father, I receive James 1:5 and come to You in the beloved name of Jesus Christ, seeking wisdom, direction, and guidance for _____.

In Jesus' name and in agreement with Luke 10:19 & 20 and Matthew 28:18, I take total authority over Satan and his demons. I command that they will become blind, deaf, and dumb to my intentional listening and prayers, and be completely removed from my presence. I also place my own thoughts and desires under Jesus' authority and command that my thoughts will obey Christ as commanded in 2 Corinthians 10:5. Please, Lord, I ask that only your Holy Spirit will speak to me as I await Your wisdom, direction, and insights for _____. And whatever You reveal and direct me to venture, I will quickly obey. Amen.

[Please note: God will never go against His Word.]

> **Set your timer & Pause for your 3-10 minutes moment of intentional listening and being with Him**
>
> ***Note: Sometimes you may not hear/see/feel anything, other times you may be overloaded with information. Either way, continue the time

with Him and watch your growth and development.

Guidance in the Silence

Even if it doesn't make sense right now, write down what you saw, heard, felt – everything, below:

_____

_____

_____

_____

_____

_____

_____

_____

_____

_____

_____

_____

Let Them Help

***Sometimes you may not fully understand what you hear/see during these times, but as you go along, what you thought was random may end up connecting and becoming a constant thread rather than a scattered appearance. Ask God for guidance and confirmation – He will show it to you.

Listening Prayer Scripture References

If any of you lacks wisdom, you should ask God, who gives generously to all without finding fault, and it will be given to you.

James 1:5

I have given you authority to trample on snakes and scorpions and to overcome all the power of the enemy; **nothing** *will harm you.[20] However, do not rejoice that the spirits submit to you, but rejoice that your names are written in heaven.*

Luke 10:19-20

Then Jesus came to them and said, "All authority in heaven and on earth has been given to me."

Matthew 28:18

We demolish arguments and every pretension that sets itself up against the knowledge of God, and we take captive every thought to make it obedient to Christ.

2 Corinthians 10:5

Turn OBSTACLE into OPPORTUNITY.

Goal #15: Resourceful

Day 15

The Good, The Bad & The Green

"The spirit of envy can destroy; it can never build."
Margaret Thatcher

God wants you: Not the you, who is trying to be someone else (though He'll love you anyway). Still, we all have had moments where we've gained a stint of envy of our friends, family, and competitors. The *trick* that will set you apart from the rest of the "envy club" is simple: *Learn from your envy*.

A few of the following responses is the typical reaction to envy:

- Having that resentment in the pit of your stomach
- Wishing it was happening to you
- Belittling the person in order to feel you have nothing to envy

- Reminding yourself that you are "way better off" as you are

Not the worst list I've seen, but usually, people stop there. One of the reactions often sustains until the next time we see something/someone worth envying. So how do we work out this jealousy for good? *By transforming envy into energy:* **Positive energy.**

You may encounter times where the feeling of envy creeps up on you, and you may not even know where it came from. Well, Miss Blessed and Highly Favored, take that feeling captive and transform it into brainstorming or working on your next idea. Allow your competitive nature to fuel your growth. The way I see it: when we become envious, it's due to either insecurity or something we haven't achieved… *yet.* Rather than sitting down in a jealous "pity pool," Love, instead, strap those 6-inch heels (or those comfy Converse kicks) and continue to work on becoming your best self. Know that just because it seems like God is doing wonders in someone else's life, doesn't mean He isn't working on your dream. God is with you every step of the way.

> **#Growth Check**
>
> **Make a list of the talents you have and those you want to achieve.** Make a plan (and stick to it) to either enhance or learn one of the skills you have on your list. Ask God to continue to show you your "sweet" spot (i.e., talent(s) in His plan). Once you re-direct envy to self-improvement and growth – you'll find that there is no longer any premise for those previous feelings to stand on.

Prayer Makes Things Happen

Dear Lord,

This may be a tough one. Lord, honestly, I sometimes look at what other people have and wonder why You haven't blessed me with it. I'm sorry that I can see things a bit shortsighted. I know and trust that You have something absolutely wonderful prepared for me. Instead of putting energy into dreaming about what others have, help me to use that energy for doing what You have for me. And when I doubt, please send Your little yet powerful reminders along the way to keep me going.

Your *loved* & *capable* daughter,

_____ (your name)

Amen

The heart of the discerning acquires knowledge, for the ears of the wise seek it out.

Proverbs 18:15

Circle for Success: *Physical*

From fitness to health to love, the physical is essential. In the Bible, our bodies are described as "temples" (1 Corinthians 6:19), and as such, this should also be a topic covered in prayer.

For this coming week, *come back to this section* and prayerfully go through your list with confidence and humility before God – and watch God work in, through and for you.

List your *physical goals* in the circle below:

Physical

Attitude + Gratitude = Aptitude

Goal #16: Thankful

Day 16

Stay Thankful

"It is not happy people who are thankful; it is thankful people who are happy."
Author Unknown

Thank God for God. Thankfulness is one of the greatest gifts He has given us. It fills us with a sense of relief and "wonder" instantaneously. One of the treasures of thankfulness is that you cannot be thankful and resentful at the same moment. Our emotions wire them differently, and it's often usually one first then the other, but non-existent simultaneously. An excellent way to begin to rid yourself of feelings of bitterness and resentment is to think, intentionally, of what you are thankful for.

I can get us started: You are currently reading – a skill that transcends vast barriers. If you are reading this or having someone read it; that means you have sight, hearing, or both, which is a wondrous blessing in itself. If the simplicity doesn't work for you, thank God for what He has for you in the near future. As a fellow or aspiring Goal Digger, you picked up this book with the ultimate move to be the boss (after God) of your own life. That alone is something to give thanks for. *You simply cannot be resentful and one hundred percent (100%) thankful at the same time.* When feelings of negativity, resentment, and bitterness arise, take time out to reflect and appreciate what you are thankful for today. And watch those pessimistic feelings begin to fade away.

#GodandtheGoalDigger Check

We talked about forming, editing, and planning your media, **now we create the content.** *Canva* is a handy tool that helps with finding free pictures, elements, and combining photos and text. This works well for those who like to use quotes or are introducing sales/deals/products for a business. *Canva* is a unique gadget, in that, the free plan has a surprisingly wide selection you can use; and when you feel like you've outgrown the free one, the paid plans give even more creative freedom and flexibility.

Prayer Makes Things Happen

Dear Heavenly Father,

God, first off, thank You. Even when I don't feel thankful, I know there are so many things to be grateful for. The fact that I'm reading this means

You have given me a new chance at life – a new day – a new beginning to make today's dream possible. Thank You for what You have brought to my life and what You will bring in the future. And in the interim, help me to continue to stay thankful for the little things and everything You bring my way.

Your *loved* & *capable* daughter,

_____ (your name)

Amen

> *Be thankful in all circumstances. This is what God wants from you in your life in union with Christ Jesus.*
>
> **1Thessalonians 5:18** (GNT)

When you make God your priority, you realize that you were His all along.

Goal #17: Re-focus

Day 17

Give it to God, Every Day

"I have nothing to worry about."
Said No Goal Digger EVER

Sometimes when we are the busiest, we are the *least* productive. Though God tells us that focusing on Him is the best thing we can do from day to day, we often feel like that isn't enough – because we aren't "doing" enough! Consistently looking to God remains one of the hardest things to accomplish. "Lord, how can I simply focus on You, when I have to figure out what I am supposed to do in my life? I feel like I'm 490378792.5 steps behind, and You ask for me to drop everything and just think of You?" .

Again, it's the hardest thing, and I can't tell you I've gotten any better, but it definitely makes sense. If you believe that God made us and that He directs our lives, then, of course, the math adds up:

Creator + Spend time with the Creator = Direction for your life

But for some reason, we get caught up in the temporary things in life that seem more urgent at the time. And though they may be worth the time, let's try not to mix up the priorities of "urgency" with the priorities of the "important." The "important" should always take precedence – even if that means making some temporary adjustments through life's everyday messes.

> **#Growth Check**
>
> **Make two lists:** one labeled *Urgent* and the other *Important*. Fill out the lists and see how you can carve time out to make the important things happen.

Prayer Makes Things Happen

Dear Lord,

This is hard for me. I say I give my cares to You but end up controlling as much as I can. Please help me to give my concerns back to You. In my hands, they are problems. But in Your hands, my worries turn to promises –promises to prosper and not to harm me, promises to give me a hope and a future (Jeremiah 9:11). I pledge to give my life to You, and when I forget this pledge, please send Your reminders throughout the day.

Your *loved* & *capable* daughter,

_____ (your name)

Amen

> *Yet the L*ORD *longs to be gracious to you; therefore he will rise up to show you compassion. For the L*ORD *is a God of justice. Blessed are all who wait for him!*
>
> Isaiah 30:18

> *Ask and it will be given to you; seek and you will find; knock and the door will be opened to you.*
>
> Matthew 7:7

Give it to God, Every Day

You are worthy.
You are worthy.
You are worthy.

Goal #18: Worth

Day 18

A Woman's Worth

"You've got to love what's yours."
Alicia Keys

You are NOT someone else's price tag. NO ONE can put a label on your worth, *except* the One to whom your worth is given. And my dear Love; God, the giver of all things worthy has deemed you priceless, invaluable and second to NONE.

As you progress on your Goal Digger journey, there will be constant pressures and opinions targeted at you: How you should market your business, who you should date, even down to what you should wear. With different people come different views and different ways of getting things done. While counsel is beneficial, *it is vital to separate opinion from truth.*

Well then, what is the truth?

1. What you do is NOT what you're worth.

Your worth is not rooted in what you do, but in who you are. Many times, people justify their value and capability by their outward successes, but the *most significant* success starts and remains within. Even when the bills aren't paid, the kids aren't cooperating or your dream hasn't yet manifested – your worth remains the same. Why? Because when God created you, He knew the *utmost* value He placed in you and what He was going to do with it. And trust me, He doesn't need any grand appeals to make it happen. Just let Him meet you where you are with full transparency. Either way – you are *His*, which means that whether you believe it or not, your worth is *unmatched*. Start seeing and receiving the woman God has valued you to be – Irreplaceable and Unstoppable.

2. As you continue to deepen your daily walk with God, He will guide you in the direction of what you stand for, who you are and who/what you are not.

A wise individual once told me that "people will always have something to say. If it's something true, *accept* it, if it's something wise, *learn* from it, but if it's something far from all the above, *throw it away!*" In essence, ultimately, you and God know what He has planned for you. On this journey, continue to ask God how to *discern* the truth from others, from yourself and then how to *refuse* the rest.

> **#GodandtheGoalDigger Check**
>
> If you're looking for a photo editor website online, you can **try out** *Online Photo Editor - Pixlr*. It has some Photoshop-esque qualities, and you can use it online for free! Another perk is that there are YouTube tutorials for this online tool as well. Soon you will be a pro - in no time at all!

Prayer Makes Things Happen

Dear Lord,

There is so much that goes on in one day. With it all, please reveal to me Your truth. I encounter so many opinions daily; I ask for Your discernment that coincides with Your will. And when it gets tough, please draw me near to You and guide me with Your wisdom and strength.

Your *loved* & *capable* daughter,

_____ (your name)

Amen

> *"I always want to stay focused on who I am, even as I'm discovering who I am."*
>
> Alicia Keys
>
> *A Woman's Worth*

God is within her, she will not fall; God will help her at break of day.

Psalm 46:5

But he said to me, "My grace is sufficient for you, for my power is made perfect in weakness." Therefore I will boast all the more gladly about my weaknesses, so that Christ's power may rest on me.

2 Corinthians 12:9

In this life, you can tear down or you can build up. The choice is yours.

Goal #19: Team

Day 19

Calm, Cool & Collaborate

"When you need to innovate, you need collaboration."
Marissa Mayer

You are a force of nature. But in today's world, everything seems like a competition. The number of start-ups is increasing; the urge for more followers on our media is intriguing, and kicking out other potential competitors, can be appealing. However, there is a difference between representing your best self and your brand and being in constant competition with those around us. To overuse the cliché again: *there is always room at the top.*

As believers in Christ, one of our core values is to lift one another up in good and godly measures. Instead of immediately jumping into "competition mode," choose to look for a way that can potentially benefit both you and the other business or person.

In a business setting, collaboration reaps more reward than competing, each time. One of the reasons why this is true is due to the power of dual forces. *The Lord says when two are in agreement*, it can lead not just to the doubling effect, but to exponential results [Matthew 18:19]. Collaborating can open countless doors for your network and business. Keeping a positive and communicatively open relationship provides potential opportunities that you wouldn't have had otherwise. If you still experience competition, instead of viewing it as a fight, think of it as iron sharpening iron: encouraging each other to be the best possible. God has space in His heart for each and every one of us. His guidance will propel us to His success and purpose for us – if we allow Him to do so.

#Growth Check

After today's **Prayer Makes Things Happen** prayer, ask God to open your mind to receive the people *He wants* you to collaborate with. Life and business can be made or broken by the influences in our lives. Ask God to bring to mind who would be the best influence and resource for your collaboration. After receiving His guidance, ask Him to confirm His choice for this venture.

Prayer Makes Things Happen

Lord,

Please give me Your eyes when choosing who to collaborate with. They say a lot of personal success and growth comes from the support circle you hang around, and I want to be the best version of who You raised me to be. I ask that You bless those who I encounter and also those You have chosen to be a part of my life – both personally and financially. Help me know when to let go and when to make things right. And please stick with me for all the in-between.

Your *loved* & *capable* daughter,

_____ (your name)

Amen

> "Collaboration is important not just because it's a better way to learn. The spirit of collaboration is penetrating every institution and all of our lives. So learning to collaborate is part of equipping yourself for effectiveness, problem-solving, innovation and life-long learning in an ever-changing networked economy."
>
> Don Tapscott

Calm, Cool & Collaborate

For just as each of us has one body with many members, and these members do not all have the same function, so in Christ we, though many, form one body, and each member belongs to all the others. We have different gifts, according to the grace given to each of us. If your gift is prophesying, then prophesy in accordance with your faith;

Romans 12:4-6

Two are better than one, because they have a good return for their labor: If either of them falls down, one can help the other up. But pity anyone who falls and has no one to help them up. Also, if two lie down together, they will keep warm. But how can one keep warm alone? Though one may be overpowered, two can defend themselves. A cord of three strands is not quickly broken.

Ecclesiastes 4:9-12

Assess
↓
Address
↓
Progress

Goal #20: Reality

Day 20

Check Your Circumstance

"You must take personal responsibility. You cannot change the circumstances, the seasons, or the wind, but you can change yourself. That is something you have charge of."
Jim Rohn

Sometimes it's just Circumstance.

Let's just admit – sometimes our mind gets ahead of us. It's like we program our mind to think the worst about people. But sometimes situations that occur between friends and associates are merely circumstantial. For example, an associate and I work in a somewhat similar field and a non-correlated set of circumstances seemed to lead him to believe that I may have been going after his clientele (to which caught me in complete shock), when in reality, the clients just happened to like both of our work and wanted different aspects of our work for their company. **Circumstantial.** Before jumping to conclusions, our best bet is to approach the person and find out for ourselves. Otherwise, we can create a problem that has no grounds.

You know that typical high school romance, where it just seems like a compilation of separate events keeping the couple from each other? Life sometimes looks like that. I'm sure we've all had our share of arguments that could have been avoided if we realized it was something that just happened on its own. And that's okay.

Not everything is circumstantial. Now if we start noticing the consistent 'circumstances' that become more of a constant routine, then it may be time to evaluate what's going on in that situation. But until then, take extra time out to see what assumptions could be reliant solely on circumstance.

> **#GodandtheGoalDigger Check**
>
> **It's time to unplug.** When you enter this Goal Digger world, there is so much being thrown at you in every direction – minimizing creativity and refreshment. Whatever unplugging looks like for you, whether that be a Mind-Cation to a Power Nap – schedule mini "Unplug sessions," that can fit any busy schedule. If it doesn't 'fit,' remind yourself of the form of productivity that comes in a four-letter word – R E S T.

Prayer Makes Things Happen

Lord,

There are a lot of things that will happen in this lifetime; some purposeful, and some out of circumstance. Please help me to decipher which is which and to better understand what's personal from what's situational. And if all else fails, please remind me that You are with me, guiding me every step of the way.

Your *loved* & *capable* daughter,

_____ (your name)

Amen

> *Let your eyes look straight ahead; fix your gaze directly before you.*
>
> **Proverbs 4:25**

> *But seek first his kingdom and his righteousness, and all these things will be given to you as well.*
>
> **Matthew 6:33**

Circle for Success: *Financial*

Ah, the most-beloved topic. Money. Money. Money. The truth is, the more we focus solely on becoming rich, the more often we fail. God says to "seek His kingdom first" (Matthew 6:33) and that everything else will fall into place. Yet often we think the opposite: that if we get our money in order first – everything else will come together. But as with all things, we don't have because we don't ask.

For this coming week, *come back to this section* and prayerfully go through your list in confidence and humility before God – and watch God work in, through and for you. Before you make your list, ask God for guidance on how to pray for your finances and how to make wise financial decisions in the future.

List your *financial goals* in the circle below:

Financial

Contrary to popular belief:
Some feelings take practice.
Do the work and feelings are bound to follow.

Goal #21: Mindset

Day 21

Mirror Check

"One of the lessons that I grew up with was to always stay true to yourself and never let what somebody else says distract you from your goals. And so when I hear about negative and false attacks, I really don't invest any energy in them, because I know who I am."
Michelle Obama

We all have that friend (or are the friend) who compares herself to other colleagues who are making their way up the success ladder. Let's call her, Petty Paula. Of course, some of us are genuinely thrilled when our friends are *killin' it* in the boss world; but in Petty Paula's eyes, she believes she won't be happy until she gets to the same spot or higher than her associates.

I completely understand girls with Petty Paula's syndrome; I once had the same diagnosis. Here's a little mental awakening that helped me get out of that deception:

1) Yours is coming – but wait, plot twist, if you spend all your energy on trying to be on the same level as your friends, then you end up

wasting effort that could have been used in full force, on your future.

2) As discussed in Day 15, this envy does more harm than good. Did you ever think that one day, you two could collaborate? Or just the mere fact that if she's your friend and you support her – when it's your time coming – she will (or at least should) be more than happy to do the same. I'm not saying to use this premise as a manipulating tool, but more of a *change of mindset*. It's very likely that when you achieve your own dream, you won't feel the same envy or resentment that you did previously, and at that "present" time you will be much more satisfied that you kept the dialogue mutually beneficial.

3) She's your FRIEND. If you are still not convinced at least consider this third option: There are sooo many other people you can strive to be like. Why choose the person you can lose a thriving relationship with when you can work on your own goals of a similar standard? Maybe your mentor should be someone even further up the success ladder – that way you can keep your competitive drive (again, if this is something that fuels you), AND maintain a happy, thriving friendship.

> **#Growth Check**
>
> **Make a list of all the positives you find in yourself and what others say about you.** If you need some help getting started, allow me: You decided to get this Goal Digger book, so I bet you're motivated or at least driving to be the bomb.com. You are currently reading this book, which means you're intelligent, and regardless of me not meeting you yet, I know that you are capable and are all the way, beautiful! After you make your list, place it somewhere where you can view it daily. Remember, Love, a positive mindset is the first step to God-confidence and accomplishing things beyond your imagination.

Prayer Makes Things Happen

Dear Lord,

Thank You for creating us for growth. I know sometimes I can get upset about some of my traits. I ask You to reveal my faults to me. Help me to see my weaknesses in a realistic lens – not in any way to put myself down, but so I can take a good look at myself and work on growth to become a better person. I know this can be challenging, but continue to encourage me that being what You have for me to be is one of the most important goals I can accomplish in this life. And for when I don't know how to move forward, please continue to show me the way.

Your *loved* & *capable* daughter,

_____ (your name)

Amen

As iron sharpens iron, so one person sharpens another.

Proverbs 27:17

Learning to Listen: The Prayer

(Adapted from Mary Geegh's *God Guides*) (Geegh, 2014)

Almighty Father, I receive James 1:5 and come to You in the beloved name of Jesus Christ, seeking wisdom, direction, and guidance for _____.

In Jesus' name and in agreement with Luke 10:19 & 20 and Matthew 28:18, I take total authority over Satan and his demons. I command that they will become blind, deaf, and dumb to my intentional listening and prayers, and be completely removed from my presence. I also place my own thoughts and desires under Jesus' authority and command that my thoughts will obey Christ as commanded in 2 Corinthians 10:5. Please, Lord, I ask that only your Holy Spirit will speak to me as I await Your wisdom, direction, and insights for _____ _____. And whatever You reveal and direct me to venture, I will quickly obey. Amen.

[Please note: God will never go against His Word.]

Set your timer & Pause for your 3-10 minutes moment of intentional listening and being with Him

***Note: Sometimes you may not hear/see/feel anything, other times you may be overloaded with information. Either way, continue the time with Him and watch your growth and development.

Guidance in the Silence

Even if it doesn't make sense right now, write down what you saw, heard, felt – everything, below:

_____

_____

_____

Mirror Check

***Sometimes you may not fully understand what you hear/see during these times, but as you go along, what you thought was random may end up connecting and becoming a constant thread rather than a scattered appearance. Ask God for guidance and confirmation – He will show it to you.

Listening Prayer Scripture References

If any of you lacks wisdom, you should ask God, who gives generously to all without finding fault, and it will be given to you.

James 1:5

I have given you authority to trample on snakes and scorpions and to overcome all the power of the enemy; **nothing** *will harm you.[20] However, do not rejoice that the spirits submit to you, but rejoice that your names are written in heaven."*

Luke 10:19-20

Then Jesus came to them and said, "All authority in heaven and on earth has been given to me."

Matthew 28:18

We demolish arguments and every pretension that sets itself up against the knowledge of God, and we take captive every thought to make it obedient to Christ.

2 Corinthians 10:5

Mirror Check

Compare who you are right now with who you want to be. Then go for it!

Goal #22: Check Yourself

Day 22

Keep Forward

"Comparison is the thief of joy."
Theodore Roosevelt

You cannot fully receive God's blessings until you stop comparing yourself to others. The left and right have NOTHING for you. When God created you, He made everything you need to maximize your goals. This tendency to compare is a daily struggle, beauties. A lot of times, we feel so overwhelmed by the success of others around us that we think God may have forgotten about us. But God continually reminds us that our blessings come "through" our *active* faith - when we believe in the things we have yet to see.

This issue has been a particular struggle for me. Here's a snippet of what I've learned from past comparisons of myself to others:

Repetitively making rounds (i.e., comparisons) to make sure we're on top:

1) Uses a lot of energy: Some days, I would compare social media profiles/ratings. Other

days if someone had something big happen for them, I would almost force something big to happen for me. Speaking from experience, this was ridiculously tiring! I am stressing right now – just thinking about it. The time I took to "keep up" ended up leaving me exhausted every day. *Once you stop looking for the approval of others through comparison (i.e. to the left or right), you will notice the wealth of energy that begins to come back into your life.*

2) **Does nothing for you:** All this time I spent comparing – didn't help. My life didn't dramatically increase during this time; the only thing it did was **take** from me. *Focus on things in your life that add that fullness to your soul and spirit – the ROI (return on investment) has a way better pay off.*

3) **Decreases happiness:** I would be so frustrated and irritated at the end of the night where all I could do was plop on my bed and go to sleep. Even the simple things used to bother me. I wonder now, *What life was I living???*

All the while, God is staring straight at you, waiting to prepare you for His blessings overflow. *When you switch the mentality of comparison and envy and focus on you, your goals and your joy – the way you look at life and better yet, the way you feel about and in your life, radically changes.* Give it a try!

#GodandtheGoalDigger Check

Don't Give Up. There will be highs and lows in your venture – celebrate the highs, learn from the lows, but don't let the lows question your capability. With the slightest tweak, an idea can turn from good to *gold*. Fail. Learn. Fail Again. Succeed!

Prayer Makes Things Happen

Dear Heavenly Father,

I know there are times when I determine success based on comparison. Lord, instead, help me to find ways that I can celebrate my milestones and to grow through my challenges. You have created me in Your eyes – a treasured *masterpiece*. Help me to always know and believe that I am treasured and loved in You.

Your *loved* & *capable* daughter,

_____ (your name)

Amen

Keep Forward

Do not conform to the pattern of this world, but be transformed by the renewing of your mind. Then you will be able to test and approve what God's will is—his good, pleasing and perfect will.

Romans 12:2

A tranquil heart gives life to the flesh, but envy makes the bones rot.

Proverbs 14:30

Each of you must examine your own actions. Then you can be proud of your own accomplishments without comparing yourself to others. Assume your own responsibility.

Galatians 6:4-5

You don't even know the half of your amazing.

Goal #23: The Power of You

Day 23

You are the Person You've Been Waiting For

"If you can dream it, you can do it."
Walt Disney

You are a *Brilliant*, *Outstanding*, *Stunning*, and *Sensational* individual, better known as a B-O-S-S. We often get this yearning for someone else to step in and tell us how we are going to set ourselves up for life. Unfortunately, not everyone is privileged to attain such counsel. And we end up looking at ourselves in the mirror, wondering what to do.

Did I say, unfortunately?? Pardon, that must've been typed by someone I used to know…. There is nothing unfortunate about having the privilege of figuring out what you want in life! There is something exciting about exploring the possibilities of what you can do! And this goes for any age. I thought by now (post-education) I would have a closer inkling of where my niche is. I am here today to tell you proudly *(maybe a bit sheepishly)* that I am still looking for where I'm supposed to be and what I am supposed to do. Instead of thinking about all the things you may not have gotten to yet, think about the new and amazing opportunities you can create for yourself!

After those long, not-so-promising days of work revisit your goals and see what you can do more of each day to achieve your passion.

#Growth Check

Don't be afraid to let your light shine. At first, this can seem like a "DUH" statement: until you start putting yourself out there and realize that you're beginning to shift the direction of your life. It is then when all the self-doubt, anxiety, and second thoughts start to cloud your mind. It is then when we grasp our stretchy jeans and walk in the God-confidence that we were meant to. It is then when we work hard and shine, bright.

Prayer Makes Things Happen

Dear Lord,

There are times where I am looking to everyone else to make my dreams possible. To be honest, sometimes, I am more afraid of trying and failing than trying at all. I want to know that it will all work and be successful before making that first step.

Please help me to get rid of the idea that everything is in my control. And better yet, continue to show me that when I put the power into Your hands, that's when things start changing for the better. Even though it may not be immediate, I put my trust in You – to take me on the journey You have set for me.

Your *loved* & *capable* daughter,

_____ (your name)

Amen

I can do all this through him who gives me strength.

Philippians 4:13

For God did not give us a spirit of timidity but one of power, love, and self-discipline.

2 Timothy 1:7

Your eyes...
Your story...

Goal #24: Secure

Day 24

Oprah Winfrey was Oprah Winfrey BEFORE becoming Oprah

*"You can either see yourself as a wave in the ocean, or you can see yourself **as** the ocean."*
Oprah Winfrey

You read it right. Oprah Winfrey was always OPRAH WINFREY. The media (for all the good and the bad) tends to glorify persons who've made it to the spotlight, giving the impression that there is some glorious algorithm for us to reach the same "greatness." And we, as a society, have bought into it. What the media neglects to mention is that there are some "Oprah Winfrey's" in our lives already. Let's not get it twisted, I chose the name Oprah Winfrey because she is on the top of my celebrity admirers list (along with Michelle Obama, Tyra Banks, Angelina Jolie, Yvonne Orji, Tamera Mowry-Housley, Jeannie Mai, Adrienne Bailon-Houghton, Loni Love, Ellen Degeneres, Issa Rae, Candace Cameron-Bure, Janelle Monae, Gal Gadot, Yara Shahidi, and the list goes on). However, there are probably a few people in your

Oprah Winfrey was Oprah Winfrey BEFORE becoming Oprah

life whose advice impacts you just as profoundly or more so, than Oprah Winfrey.

Point: Oprah was always Oprah. The only difference between Oprah Winfrey and the people who significantly impact your life is that more people take notice of her.

Do not let outside influences affect your value. *Be the Oprah Winfrey of your own life.* There wasn't a pinpoint in time of Oprah's life where she finally "became" herself - because she was always and will always be, Oprah. In short, my dears, you have all that you need for greatness already instilled inside of you. First, you have to believe it, and then, *grow* it.

> **#GodandtheGoalDigger Check**
>
> **You've got Mail.** From Entrepreneur to 9 to 5, having a professional email persona is another step to representing you. Gmail from Google is a free sign up service that gives you an option of forming a business email along with a business setup. If you're looking to go further with pictures and personalized branding, though not free, *MailChimp* is one of the many providers with a manageable setup and reasonable prices. Having a more professional appearance not only helps engage your customers, but it reminds us that we are the do, or die, of our brand. Let's do!

Prayer Makes Things Happen

Dear Lord,

I am not Oprah Winfrey. Nor do I need to be. You have already decided on my purpose and placed all the wonder and talent inside of me. I continue to put my trust in You to help me cultivate those talents, so that when You are ready to bless me with the results – I will be ready. In the meantime, please stick with me - remind me in Your way that I am beloved, treasured and have the same "thing" that celebrities all around the world have. More so,

Oprah Winfrey was Oprah Winfrey BEFORE becoming Oprah

confirm to me that I have *You;* and that beats worldly expectations any and every day.

Your *loved* & *capable* daughter,

_____ (your name)

Amen

> *I praise you because I am fearfully and wonderfully made; your works are wonderful, I know that full well.*
>
> Psalm 139:14

very day is an opportunity to create cause for celebration.

Goal #25: Appreciate

Day 25

Make Your Own Adventure

"Every day of your life is a special occasion."
Thomas S. Monson

I said it. The status quo at the moment encourages us to "hurry up and get it," and for the most part, we listen to every word of it. But the truth is life will never be EXACTLY where we want it to be. So what do we do? We make celebratory moments for life along the way. You "killed" that event? Yes, Love, let's cheer – to you! You got all of your kids to bed on time? OMG! Miracle-worker! You hit 1000 views on YouTube? Yes, Yes, Yes!

Before this new mindset, I had a habit of constantly downing myself to do better. If I did fifty (50) things right in a day and one (1) wrong, I was pin-focused on that wrong item for the rest of the day - until I found a way to fix it. Yes, on the one hand, I figured out how to resolve the problem. But, on the other hand, I spent too much valuable time stressing about one imperfection. I've finally realized that life is packed with little flaws, but when compared to the whole, they are still worth celebrating.

And amazingly, sometimes those imperfections end up not being imperfections at all.

A Mini Story with a Meaning

The photographer in me was taking pictures of a client, and when I got home to look at the originals, I realized that there was this smoky glare in most of the images. Of course, my first reaction was, "Gahh! What's wrong with me? Why didn't I check the camera lens before taking pictures??" Nevertheless, I still attempted to edit them normally. When I got to the editing, I realized that the smoky glare instead *added* more depth and mystery to the picture – the precise angle the client was going for!!!

The moral of my mini-tangent, *By stressing about every little thing that goes awry in our lives, we can miss out on something better that God has for us.* He turned my "mistake" into creative art. Imagine what He can do with your not-so-perfect moments.

> **#Growth Check**
>
> **Through it all..., be Kind.** Times may get rough, but a soft heart will always grow and rise above. I could not write another page in this book without letting Maya Angelou (may her soul rest in peace), speak:
>
> > *"People will forget what you said, people will forget what you did, but people will never forget how you made them feel."*
>
> After it's all said and done, how you will be remembered depends significantly upon the actions you choose today. *Make them Count!*

Prayer Makes Things Happen

Lord,

Life gets messy. Though I would love life going my way, I know that I cannot always be in control of my circumstances. Lord, help me to lean on You and hear Your voice on how to go through this life adventure. And even when it doesn't feel like an adventure, help me to see past the tough days for Your glory. I ask that You grant me special moments, even amidst the imperfections.

Your *loved* & *capable* daughter,

_____ (your name)

Amen

> *Do not be anxious about anything, but in every situation, by prayer and petition, with thanksgiving, present your requests to God.*
>
> *And the peace of God, which transcends all understanding, will guard your hearts and your minds in Christ Jesus.*
>
> Philippians 4: 6-7

Circle for Success: *Emotional*

I long for the day where I am so emotionally sound that I have a calculated, godly response for every encounter. Until then, let's pray for it and each other. Some of my emotional goals are: to completely trust God, to wholeheartedly love others with God's love, but also with the discernment to know what's good from the not-so-good in my life.

For this coming week, *come back to this section* and prayerfully go through your list with confidence and humility before God – and watch God work in, through and for you.

List your *emotional goals* in the circle below:

Emotional

Do you ever think sometimes we just get it wrong?

Goal #26: Perspective

Day 26

The Glass Half Full

"If everything was perfect, you would never learn and you would never grow."
Beyoncé

Today I met a gentleman who has no home, and I'm the one who benefitted from it. A couple of my friends were getting their nails done (but I was "being cheap" at the time), so I headed over to the Publix nearby. While I was on the phone, the young gentleman asked if I had any food.

Side-note

(You can skip the side-note if you are too eager to see what happens.) I know there are a plethora of social issues and problems in the world, but homelessness hits home (probably not the best place for a pun). REDO ~~homelessness hits home~~ → homelessness wrings my heart. I cannot fathom the anxiety of not knowing where your next meal is coming from, where you are going to lay your head at night, or where to get more water. No matter how much we can pair up with organizations, it never seems to be enough.

Apologies, *back to the point* (thanks for coming to my TED talk): The young gentleman asked if I had any food. I politely shook my head *(saying no)* and apologized for it, but noticed there was a restaurant on the other side of the nail salon. So I caught up with him and told him we could have lunch over there. After I'd purchased his lunch and we finished up, I asked him if there was anything else he needed or wanted. He responded, "Nah, thank you so much, but I have all that I need."

I can't even….

When you have already been blessed with the essentials of life (air, food, water, shelter) – even remotely – we tend to end up complaining more because we have been accustomed to our needs being met – automatically!

Still, in the midst of all the uncertainty and unknown, the young gentlemen responded, "**I have all that I need.**"

Long story for a short pause: Don't let the dictations of others determine your joy. Figure out *what brings you joy* and set that as your "making it" goal. For the young gentleman, it was a meal for

GOD AND THE GOAL DIGGER

the day; for me (in progress), it's knowing that I am where God wants me to be *(a divine appointment)*.

Find out what really gives you that extra oomph and work towards it.

We receive God's Blessings for you, In Jesus' name.

#Growth Check

Write down ten (10) main things you are thankful for. Read them each day and remember to thank God for what He has already given you and for what's to come. Be mindful that God is the supplier of our *needs;* the rest is just gravy (aka extra). A thankful heart will reap more blessings than we can imagine. **Stay thankful.**

Prayer Makes Things Happen

Dear Lord,

One of the key things I would like to leave with after this journey is *thankfulness*. I can get so focused on the specifics of life that I often forget how to be genuinely thankful. Lord, please bless my heart with gratefulness and gratitude to renew my mindset to one of joy, peace and hope.

The Glass Half Full

Your *loved* & *capable* daughter,

_____ (your name)

Amen

> *Therefore do not worry, saying, 'What shall we eat?' or 'What shall we drink?' or 'What shall we wear?' For the pagans pursue all these things, and your Heavenly Father knows that you need them. But seek first the kingdom of God and His righteousness, and all these things will be added unto you.*
>
> **Matthew 6:32, 33** (Study Bible)

f you can break down your ultimate
goals into smaller actionable ones,
Love, you can do anything.

Goal #27: Management

Day 27

Hakuna Matata

"You only live once, but if you do it right, once is enough."
Mae West

Sometimes when life gets too overwhelming, it can be an incredible relief to just focus on what's right in front of you. This is not negating future plans at all; in fact, often looking at what's right in front of you helps you better prepare for the future. Currently, I have little idea what's going on in my life.

Here are the things I am currently certain of:

1. God
2. My Family
3. Lemon Water

I would "drain" myself every day – trying to figure out the answer(s) to my uncertain life. It wasn't until I brought my 5-year plan into segments of 3-9-2-7-4-2-6 everyday plans (you get the gist), that I began to gain energy and momentum. If you can work on looking at tomorrow's agenda, or better yet, today's, and move forward, you'll be surprised how much more energy and positivity your life will embrace.

> **#GodandtheGoalDigger Check**
>
> **Website Time.** Depending on your craft, a website can be helpful to have; it's a place your media can be directed to, but what also can be used as a consistent portfolio and representation of what you stand for. Take some time to flesh out your ideas, and in the interim, there are many free website starters: *Wix.com, Wordpress.com*, etc. Or you can go straight to having your own domain by upgrading to one of their paid plans or another program *like Squarespace. Squarespace* is one of the growing and leading website interfaces and has a spread of modern and clean designs with great mobile compatibility. Here are the basic pros and cons (gathered from **personal use**).
>
> **Wix**
>
> *Pros:* Easy to use/maneuver
>
> *Cons:* The mobile compatibility lags longer than other programs
>
> **Wordpress**
>
> *Pros:* Great custom coding ability
>
> *Cons:* Ready-made, layout themes can look a bit outdated

> **Squarespace**
>
> *Pros:* Affordable, modern, clean layouts
>
> *Cons:* Choice of layouts limited

Prayer Makes Things Happen

Dear Heavenly Father,

On the topic of gratitude, I ask that You help me find tangible ways to give and practice thankfulness. The Bible encourages cheerful giving, and as such, please bless my spirit with joy and discernment when giving to myself and others. Train my attitude in the way that I respond. May it be according to Your faithfulness and truth. In times of struggle remind me that a touch of thankfulness can extend to everlasting rewards. Thank You for the ability to be thankful.

Your *loved* & *capable* daughter,

_____ (your name)

Amen

> *Therefore do not worry about tomorrow, for tomorrow will worry about itself. Each day has enough trouble of its own.*
>
> Matthew 6:34

Hakuna Matata

When God's plans for your life come knocking, will you be ready to answer the door?

Goal #28: Flexibility

Day 28

The Little Things are the Big Things

> *"True greatness consists in being great in little things."*
> **Charles Simmons**

I was visiting a church back in my hometown (Nassau, Bahamas), and the pastor's message stuck with me. In a world of "Think Big, Dream Big, Do Big," I was intrigued to hear that his conclusion was to stop big thinking. Are you telling me, Adria Brooke McCardy (aka Adria Bee), that I cannot dream big???! How my life was potentially turned upside down.

The more I continued to listen, the more it made sense.... He said stop big thinking *so you can start enjoying the little things*. In my interpretation, he doesn't mean literally to stop thinking big – his emphasis was more on being able to enjoy the little things that God takes us through along the journey. That and the big plans we have for ourselves may not necessarily be God's plans.

Can you imagine pursuing something for a lifetime and it never comes to fruition? We get frustrated and ask God why us, when God may have been trying to tell us that's *not* our success path all along. Sometimes thinking big and setting out personal plans on our lives may be the opposite of where God wants to take us. Rather, if we focus on the everyday little things, we not only experience a fuller, joyful life but also make more room for the blessings God is ready to share with us. (Thanks, pastor.) Again, it isn't about not thinking big - think big! But while you are thinking big, remember God is subject to redefine what that "big" truly means.

#GodandtheGoalDigger Check

Are you proclaiming your goals each day? When I was in college, I wrote a five (5) million-dollar check on my wall. I eyed (sometimes kissed) the check every day until I started to make things happen.

However, it's essential to watch your heart. There is a difference between having a goal and having a "*greed.*" As *I needed to do*, shift your goal to first and foremost, *God's plan* – in whatever form that may be – while letting God know your desires. In time and growth in Him, your wishes will align, and true success will be around the corner.

> *#Note:* Sometimes, we think if we trust God with our lives, it won't be the type of experience we wanted (e.g., wealth, fame, etc.). But that is simply a clear sign of how *little* trust we have in Him. God is a God of no limits. Imagine what He can do with your life – if only given a chance.

Prayer Makes Things Happen

Dear Lord,

Please help me take in and embrace the little things. I am a dreamer and a go-getter, but I still want to see the joy and blessings in the everyday little things. Let me meet You in the moments of celebration when You bring the small but significant blessings from day to day; prepare me so that I will be ready and able to receive the big ones too. I can often feel timid about requesting these things, but the Bible encourages us to ask for what we want to see in our lives. Therefore, I pray that these blessings are according to Your good and perfect will.

Your *loved* & *capable* daughter,

_____ (your name)

Amen

The Little Things are the Big Things

One who is faithful in very little is also faithful in much.

Luke 16:10a (ESV)

Learning to Listen: The Prayer

(Adapted from Mary Geegh's *God Guides*) (Geegh, 2014)

Almighty Father, I receive James 1:5 and come to You in the beloved name of Jesus Christ, seeking wisdom, direction, and guidance for _____.

In Jesus' name and in agreement with Luke 10:19 & 20 and Matthew 28:18, I take total authority over Satan and his demons. I command that they will become blind, deaf, and dumb to my intentional listening and prayers, and be completely removed from my presence. I also place my own thoughts and desires under Jesus' authority and command that my thoughts will obey Christ as commanded in 2 Corinthians 10:5. Please, Lord, I ask that only your Holy Spirit will speak to me as I await Your wisdom, direction, and insights for _____ _____. And whatever You reveal and direct me to venture, I will quickly obey. Amen.

[*Please note: God will never go against His Word.*]

Set your timer & Pause for your 3-10 minutes moment of intentional listening and being with Him

***Note: Sometimes you may not hear/see/feel anything, other times you may be overloaded with information. Either way, continue the time with Him and watch your growth and development.

Guidance in the Silence

Even if it doesn't make sense right now, write down what you saw, heard, felt – everything, below:

_____
_____
_____
_____
_____
_____
_____
_____
_____

The Little Things are the Big Things

***Sometimes you may not fully understand what you hear/see during these times, but as you go along, what you thought was random may end up connecting and becoming a constant thread rather than a scattered appearance. Ask God for guidance and confirmation – He will show it to you.

Listening Prayer Scripture References

> *If any of you lacks wisdom, you should ask God, who gives generously to all without finding fault, and it will be given to you.*
>
> James 1:5

> *I have given you authority to trample on snakes and scorpions and to overcome all the power of the enemy;* **nothing** *will harm you.[20] However, do not rejoice that the spirits submit to you, but rejoice that your names are written in heaven."*
>
> Luke 10:19-20

> *Then Jesus came to them and said, "All authority in heaven and on earth has been given to me.*
>
> Matthew 28:18

> *We demolish arguments and every pretension that sets itself up against the knowledge of God, and we take captive every thought to make it obedient to Christ.*
>
> 2 Corinthians 10:5

If faith were easy, it'd be spelled L-A-Z-Y.

Goal #29: Change

Day 29

My Favorite "F" Word

"Faith is taking the first step even when you don't see the whole staircase."
Martin Luther King, Jr.

Saying thanks after something happens *isn't* faith, it's gratitude. Faith is saying thanks *before* the result occurs; better known as claiming it (Warren, 2019).

If there is anything I've learned on the entrepreneurship road, it is that you can't be nearsighted. *It wasn't until I started to believe in the things I couldn't see that I saw a positive change in my life.* Even if you aren't a believer, faith is having hope for the future and the willpower and trust to make it happen. *In order to go further than you've ever been, you have to believe in something greater than you've ever done.* That, my friend, is the recipe for growth. And faith is a significant aspect of this growth. Most celebrity powerhouses you see today all had their moments where they thought their dreams were just that – dreams. Yet they pressed on, having faith in the reality that did not yet exist, and they *made* it! Now it's your turn.

> **#GodandtheGoalDigger Check**
>
> **From now on, let's do a vocabulary check:** turn your "can't" to "will" and your "try" to "did" – then watch how much your life takes its course.

Prayer Makes Things Happen

Lord,

Faith is one of the hardest parts of life to achieve. Sure, we can all speak positivity and direction over our lives, but believing and acting on it is another level. I ask You that You grant me the gift of *faith*. Teach me how to speak faith and life into my livelihood and to proclaim Your will for me. Allow my faith to be so full that it flows into the lives of all those around me. Even now, when I cannot see what You have in store, wrap me in Your loving arms and remind me that my blessings overflow is coming.

Your *loved* & *capable* daughter,

_____ (your name)

Amen

*But they who wait for the L*ORD *shall renew their strength; they shall mount up with wings like eagles; they shall run and not be weary; they shall walk and not faint.*

Isaiah 40:31 (ESV)

Now faith is the substance of things hoped for, the evidence of things not seen.

Hebrews 11:1 (KJV)

hen you finally understand who God is and who He made you to be, you'll be unstoppable.

Goal #30: Seek

Day 30

Watch God Instead of People

"Confidence is not 'they will like me.' Confidence instead is 'I'll be fine if they don't.'"
Christina Grimmie

No need to worry about what anyone else is doing. Sometimes we feel like we aren't going anywhere if the people surrounding us are doing "better." But God has never left us. God has never left *you*. He wants to overwhelm you with His blessings and kindness. He wants to show you His love over and over again. He is simply waiting for you, my dear!

When the situations of others consume us, we often neglect to focus on ourselves, or furthermore, focusing on God – the only One who knows what great things He has for you. Yes, it's definitely a struggle to keep reminding yourself of the reality that there is something (or someone) you cannot necessarily see. But darling, that doesn't mean it isn't there. *Look again*…, and again after that. I promise you, if you keep redirecting your thoughts towards God instead of people, your life (and how you look at it) will change for the better.

> **#Growth Check**
>
> When you start to look over your shoulder to see what everyone else is doing, **remind yourself of the many things that you are thankful for.** Then remind yourself of who God is. Here are a few names He goes by. *Provider. Healer. Omnipotent.* He makes nothing half-way: especially when referring to *you*.
>
> - *Do the Work.*
> - *Love on Yourself.*
> - *Watch God.*

Prayer Makes Things Happen

Dear Lord,

Life is full of distractions. I often get deep in the thoughts and actions of others and make it my duty to control or fix what they think of me. Help me to remember that what *You* think of me is the most important part of my testimony. Some of the thoughts You've shared with me are that I am powerful, confident, unique, treasured and loved. Even when I don't portray some of these attributes

– remind me *Whose* I am and that I can do all things through Your strength (Phil 4:13). Help me to look to You first and to let that guide my decisions daily.

Your *loved* & *capable* daughter,

_____ (your name)

Amen

> *Be strong and courageous. Do not be afraid or terrified because of them, for the Lord your God goes with you; he will never leave you nor forsake you.*
>
> Deuteronomy 31:6

Circle for Success: *Spiritual*

I can hear you now:

"Adria, if this is a devotional, why is the most important aspect of your book (spiritual) coming near the end of the Circle for Success goals?"

Thank you for asking. I placed the Spiritual Circle for Success goal near the end for a very simple reason: Spirituality is complex. A lot of times we don't feel connected to God not because we aren't working on our spiritual connection, but because we have been neglecting the other aspects of our lives (emotional, physical, etc.) that build up to spirituality.

What we emotionally and physically feed into our lives will respectively affect how we approach our spiritual lives.

For this coming week, *come back to this section* and prayerfully go through your list with confidence and humility before God – and watch God work in, through and for you.

List your *spiritual* (in God) *goals* in the circle below:

Spiritual

Trust the process.
Trust **is** a process.

Goal #31: Trust

Day 31

Trust God

"The best proof of love is trust."
Joyce Brothers

There is one thing to watch God, and another, to trust Him. Trusting God requires belief and the proclamation that He has good for your life – in all stages. It's easy to commit to this when everything is on the up and up. However, if you can master trusting God during the phases of the not-so-good moments, you will be surprised how your faith is strengthened and how it prepares you for future triumphs as you face various trials in your life.

A little goes a *long* way. When my journey of trusting God first started, I began to give Him my trust in small things: such as getting through workouts and trusting Him to help me accomplish my tasks for the day. As I began to see and experience God's unwavering presence, it became easier to trust him with the bigger aspects of my life *(even though at times this can still be quite challenging)*.

In the process of gym weight training, if you gradually increase weights as you go along, rather than go to the heaviest barbell weights at first, you'll be surprised at how much strength you've gained in those increments. Likewise, God doesn't expect you to be able to trust Him with your life one hundred percent (100%) – all the time – every day and minute of the week, but to be open about the possibility of giving Him a little more, each day.

> **#GodandtheGoalDigger Check**
>
> **Body. Mind. Spirit.** All of these are seen as the temple to glorify God. While we are working on our mind and spirit through this time together, what are you doing for your body? There's a reason why making healthier choices helps us with our overall mood. God designed us to be completely "healthy" in Him. Our health choices are just another step in the direction of getting ready for success. Even if it's as simple as reducing sugar intake and increasing our water consumption, you'll be surprised how a little change can make a big difference.

Prayer Makes Things Happen

Dear Lord,

Where there is faith, there is trust. Help me to trust in You. So many others have broken me down that I need help to learn how to trust You fully all over again. Thank You for giving me the wonderful opportunity of having a relationship with You. I ask that You heal me of all that may hinder my total trust in You.

Your *loved* & *capable* daughter,

_____ (your name)

Amen

> *Trust in the LORD with all your heart, and do not lean on your own understanding. In all your ways acknowledge him, and he will make straight your paths.*
>
> Proverbs 3:5-6 (ESV)

Just your daily reminder that when
life happens,
God isn't going anywhere.

Goal #32: Consistency

Day 32

Watch God Again

"Never let a bad day make you feel like you have a bad life."
Anonymous (but wise)

The devil was BUSY today! Here I am working on Day 32 and feeling good about myself.

"Yessss, I don't need to watch anybody, I'm watching God's glory and loving it!!!"

Until something clicked my emotional trigger – And my Love – All belief flew out the window!

> ***Pet Peeve:** What saddens me is when you are the giver in relationships, friendships, or business connections, everything is readily received, but little is reciprocated (or none for that matter). I'm not saying that you should give to receive or that every action needs to have a similar corresponding one; but I'm sure most of us have been in the position where the people in our lives show minimal support for us personally, but go above, and beyond the extra mile for people they just met or aren't even that connected to. ***Taking a deep breath***

Okay back to me being a 'good Christian' and watching God.... I needed to remind myself that God is my way-maker and not people. God is YOUR way-maker. When you get off track throughout the day, take a breather and refresh yourself with God's promises → He will provide for you. All things work together for His good; He most certainly knows the plans He has for you.

> **#Growth Check**
>
> **At the end of this chapter are some of God's promises to review,** especially when you get in those ruts and dry spells. Commit them to memory so that your heart can recall them on the spot (when needed).

Prayer Makes Things Happen

Dear Heavenly Father,

You are good. The days can be so full that I sometimes forget Your goodness and control of my life. When pressure comes, guide me in Your loving spirit. Remind me that what people do on an earthly level, You can transform on a heavenly level. If I keep my eyes focused on You I cannot imagine how much my life can change for the better. Show me how.

Your *loved* & *capable* daughter,

_____ (your name)

Amen

GOD'S PROMISES

>I will guide you along the best pathway for your life. I will advise you and watch over you.
>
>>Psalm 32:8 (NLT)
>
>Faith assures us of things we expect and convinces us of the existence of things we cannot see.
>
>>Hebrews 11:1 (GW)
>
>You keep him in perfect peace whose mind is stayed on you, because he trusts in you.
>
>>Isaiah 26:3
>
>[I] will be with you wherever you go.
>
>>Joshua 1:9
>
>*For I know the plans I have for you, plans to prosper you and not to harm you, plans to you hope and a future.*
>
>>Jeremiah 29:11

In the morning, LORD, you hear my voice; in the morning, I lay my requests before you and wait expectantly.

Psalm 5:3

I consider that our present sufferings are not worth comparing with the glory that will be revealed in us.

Romans 8:18

*I praise you because I am fearfully and **wonderfully** made; your works are wonderful, I know that full well.*

Psalm 139:14

*But he said to me, my grace is sufficient for you, for my power is **made perfect** in weakness." Therefore, I will boast all the more gladly about my weaknesses, so that Christ's power may rest on me. That is why, for Christ's sake, I **delight** in weaknesses, in insults, in hardships, in persecutions, in difficulties. For when I am weak, then I am strong.*

2nd Corinthians 12:9-11

*The LORD makes firm the steps of the one who **delights** in him; though he may stumble, he will **not** fall, for the LORD upholds him with his hand.*

Psalm 37:23-24

God can do anything, you know – far more than you could ever imagine or guess or request in your wildest dreams! He does it not by pushing us around but by working within us, his Spirit deeply and gently working within us.

Ephesians 3:20 (MSG)

Always remember what is written in this book. Study it day and night to be sure to obey everything that is written there. If you do this, you will be wise and successful in **everything**.

Joshua 1:8 (NCV)

According to your faith let it be done to you.

Matthew 9:29b

I've banked your promises in the vault of my heart.

Psalm 119:11 (MSG)

When you know yourself,
you are making the decision to
choose what happens in your life -
not just letting life happen to you.

Goal #33: Self-Discovery

Day 33

Know Your Triggers

"Take control of your consistent emotions and begin to consciously and deliberately reshape your daily experience of life."
Tony Robbins

Emotional trigger: an occurrence that easily elicits/brings up familiar emotions such as pain, joy, etc. Take the time to know your triggers. Some of mine, off the top of my head, are public bathrooms, FOMO (fear of missing out syndrome), and superficiality (i.e., flakiness). Instead of meandering throughout the day feeling irritated and not knowing exactly why, spend a few minutes here assessing your emotional triggers. And the next time one hits you, you will be better prepared to acknowledge the trigger, evaluate the cause of your emotion, slap some Jesus on the situation and resolve it, moving forward.

List some of your Emotional Triggers below:

_____

_____

_____

_____

_____

_____

_____

#GodandtheGoalDigger Check

Create your own lane. What works for someone else may not work for you. Trying to fit a title that is not for you is like you wearing a bigger shoe size (which by the way is very uncomfortable and irritating to the feet). Yes, it may "work," but it just doesn't feel natural. Even while creating your lane, there will be things you don't want to do. The difference is: being able to do what you genuinely want to do will make the things you don't like to do that much easier. From Mamahood to business and all the in-betweens…make sure the path you're on is YOURS – but most importantly make sure God's on the path with you.

Prayer Makes Things Happen

Lord,

In today's world, everything is a potential trigger. Help me to understand what makes me "tick" and learn how to handle those moments as You would have me to do. Thank You for giving us a variety of emotions and ways to embrace and express them. When that trigger hits, please help me to seek You first before giving in to negativity. Thank You for your covering.

Your *loved* & *capable* daughter,

_____ (your name)

Amen

> *And the peace of God, which surpasses all comprehension, will guard your hearts and your minds in Christ Jesus.*
>
> Philippians 4:7

Shake it off, Love.
A new day is on the horizon.

Goal #34: Perseverance

Day 34

New Day. Who Dis? Taking Each Day as it Comes

"You cry and you scream and you stomp your feet and you shout. You say, 'You know what? I'm giving up, I don't care.' And then you go to bed and you wake up and it's a brand new day, and you pick yourself back up again."
Nicole Scherzinger

The good thing about yesterday is that it was yesterday – you can't go back and rearrange how you would have preferred the day to go. The good news…EVERY new day is a chance to do even better than yesterday. There is a time to dwell on our past failures, but there is also a time to fail, shrug it off, and get ready for the new day – a new day filled with opportunities and blessings at the ready. A new day, to me, represents hope and a fresh perspective that yesterday didn't bring. Embracing each day as it comes sets your mind up for success, and your heart ready to receive it.

Do you know our God? God can turn your life story around in a matter of minutes, seconds –

milliseconds even. Imagine what He can do when given a full day! *Go into each day embracing new opportunities and shrugging off the failures of yesterday.*

Give your day to Him.

#Growth Check

There will always be two (2) people with you for the rest of your life.

1. God

2. You

Speak to yourself with kindness, confidence, positivity, and a WHOLE lot of love and watch your thoughts follow. I like to refer to myself as "baby, sweet love, boo thang" etc. because I know that the way I talk/think to myself, will translate into every other action I pursue. The way you love others is often a reflection of how you feel about yourself. One of the main things I hope you take away from this book is to *take the time out to get to know, love, cherish, and be yourself.* I guarantee it will be one of the most impactful decisions of your life.

Prayer Makes Things Happen

Dear Heavenly Father,

Lord, we know You direct our ways. Remind us that every day is an opportunity to do better than the day before. Please give us the strength, courage, and peace of mind for whatever You have for us to face each day. Thank You for all of Your goodness and grace.

Thank You for giving us the ability to choose. Help me to choose each day as a new opportunity to explore and achieve. When one day doesn't work out as I wanted it to, I ask for gratitude and hope for future days to come. Remind me that no day is a perfect day and regardless, Your love will carry me through each and every day.

Your *loved* & *capable* daughter,

_____ (your name)

Amen

> "For I know the plans I have for you," declares the LORD, "plans to prosper you and not to harm you, plans to give you hope and a future.""
>
> Jeremiah 29:11

Important
over
Impressive

Goal #35: What Counts

Day 35

Think About Forever

"Our greatest danger in life is permitting the urgent things to crowd out the important."
Charles E. Hummel

If best friends were predicted by the amount of time you spend with someone, my phone would win – every time. It has gotten to the extent that I now make a mental note to put my phone face down when I don't want to miss out on something going on around me. Being in the media field and managing small companies has only increased my mobile usage, and I constantly remind myself that *the world will not turn over if I turn my phone off* once in a while.

Featuring Now vs. Forever:

When my phone rings or dings, I sense its immediate pull for me to check out what's been going on. It sure feels like forever when I don't check my updates, but we all know ninety-eight (98%) of the time, our phone/media notifications are not urgent. In this fast-paced life, we can either live as if everything needs to be sorted now, or start to have a mental prioritization: separating the urgencies from the important.

Urgent

There are a lot of surprises that enter our lives that need our immediate attention: messy spills, deadlines, fixes, emergency calls, etc. And while they cannot necessarily be put on hold, our attitude certainly needs to have an aptitude that responds to change. While you may not be able to re-schedule what you have to do, you can control how you react to those around you. A simple, "Thank you for your patience, something has come up, and unfortunately, I won't be able to...," will be taken much more admirably than the short, "I can't respond," (or worse, no response at all).

Being aware of my reactions has not only given me more peace, but it has helped keep good mutual relationships with friends and clients alike. Remember *Wonder Women...*, the recurring question to ask ourselves is, "How am I living?" Make this inquiry if we wish to optimize the lives we want to live.

Important

Truthfully, as I was writing this same section, one of my loved ones came to the door. Now you and I have been conversing with each other for a while now, and I think you can agree – we are ladies who like to get things DONE. So, of course, I was religiously tempted to tell my loved one to wait just a bit longer so I could finish some work – but I didn't.

The truth is, there will always be something "urgent" to attend to; the issue forms when our urgencies overthrow the *important* things each time. My top love language (in *The 5 Love Languages* by **Gary Chapman**) (Chapman, 1995) is quality time. Therefore, it's crucial that I set aside time to refresh and refill my love tank so that I can continue to express love and kindness to others.

Don't focus on the "need to do right now" *so much* that you forget to enjoy the moments that lead to forever.

#GodandtheGoalDigger Check

If you are expanding your business/brand on social media, **invest in a decent picture-editing software or program.** *Instagram's* editing (alongside the filter option), has most of the features you would use in an editing program, but unfortunately, it's not made for other media platforms. Most photographers use *Adobe Photoshop* or *Adobe Lightroom*; both have the ability to edit camera pictures in

> *raw* form, giving you more depth and flexibility in your photos. If you are taking pictures with your phone, you can use the free editing app *Snapseed* or other paid apps such as Facetune, etc.

Prayer Makes Things Happen

Dear Lord,

When it comes to important versus urgent, urgent wins hands down. I ask that You help reframe my mindset to make time for the important aspects of my life that I may not be giving the needed time to. Help me to handle the urgencies in a way that doesn't neglect the essential things, but still allows me to make remedies for the situation. Through everything, thank You for being patient with us. May Your goodness overflow onto us; allowing us to set the example You set before us to others.

Your *loved* & *capable* daughter,

_____ (your name)

Amen

Set your minds on things above, not on earthly things.

Colossians 3:2

Circle for Success: *Mental*

You made it, Love! *The Last Circle Topic* before the finale. Whatever you do, don't skip this one. Everything that we do in life starts with our mindset. From our minds to our hearts, we want to be the best that God has made us to be. As such, we also need to focus on where our mindset is. Take a moment and assess all you've been telling yourself: what you can do, what you cannot do, and the reason(s) behind it. If you see a blockage somewhere in your life, there is a high chance that there is a *blocking mindset* behind it. If you're not sure where the blocking mindset is, pray and ask God to reveal it to you this week.

Let's finish strong – Prayerfully List your ideal *mental goals* and proclaim Your blessings in the circle on the next page:

Think About Forever

Mental

Learning to Listen: The Prayer

(Adapted from Mary Geegh's *God Guides*) (Geegh, 2014)

Almighty Father, I receive James 1:5 and come to You in the beloved name of Jesus Christ, seeking wisdom, direction, and guidance for _____.

In Jesus' name and in agreement with Luke 10:19 & 20 and Matthew 28:18, I take total authority over

Satan and his demons. I command that they will become blind, deaf, and dumb to my intentional listening and prayers, and be completely removed from my presence. I also place my own thoughts and desires under Jesus' authority and command that my thoughts will obey Christ as commanded in 2 Corinthians 10:5. Please, Lord, I ask that only your Holy Spirit will speak to me as I await Your wisdom, direction, and insights for _____ _____. And whatever You reveal and direct me to venture, I will quickly obey. Amen.

[Please note: God will never go against His Word.]

Set your timer & Pause for your 3-10 minutes moment of intentional listening and being with Him

> ***Note: Sometimes you may not hear/see/feel anything, other times you may be overloaded with information. Either way, continue the time with Him and watch your growth and development.

Guidance in the Silence

Even if it doesn't make sense right now, write down what you saw, heard, felt – everything, below:

_____

_____

_____

_____

_____

_____

_____

_____

_____

***Sometimes you may not fully understand what you hear/see during these times, but as you go along, what you thought was random may end up connecting and becoming a constant thread rather than a scattered appearance. Ask God for guidance and confirmation – He will show it to you.

Listening Prayer Scripture References

If any of you lacks wisdom, you should ask God, who gives generously to all without finding fault, and it will be given to you.

James 1:5

I have given you authority to trample on snakes and scorpions and to overcome all the power of the enemy; **nothing** *will harm you.[20] However, do not rejoice that the spirits submit to you, but rejoice that your names are written in heaven."*

Luke 10:19-20

Then Jesus came to them and said, "All authority in heaven and on earth has been given to me.

Matthew 28:18

We demolish arguments and every pretension that sets itself up against the knowledge of God, and we take captive every thought to make it obedient to Christ.

2 Corinthians 10:5

Think About Forever

Real confidence lies in who you are, not what you wear.

Goal #36: Priorities

Day 36

More Shorts and a Tee

"The more you like yourself, the less you are like anyone else, which makes you unique."
Walt Disney

Listen. I had a constant need to impress others with what I wore. Not because we're all fashionistas in our own right (even though we are *snap snap*), but because I felt like I was always in the midst of a "whose car is bigger," subtle conversations. So yes, I dressed the part and even wanted to hear feedback from it. The days I did get those compliments gave me an extra boost; the days I didn't, it saddened me and got me wondering, "Did I flop today?"

In reality, the pressure to dress up *didn't* come from anyone but myself. Sure, there will always be something said (or unsaid) that can cause pressure, but the real struggle came from within me and my not-so-friendly, insecurities. I really had to sit down and assess, "What the f... frig... he... heck was I doing?!?"

The moment you base your success and happiness on the opinions of others is the moment you fail (yourself). I had to come to Jesus swiftly! How dare I put so much power into the hands of others! Do you know how dangerous that is? People – people who you don't know if they have your best interest at heart, are the same persons you are allowing to rate your daily decisions?

Girl, forever Bye.

Anyway, why is this topic more shorts and a tee? ...Because, as we continue to work on our insecurities, our self-worth and self-confidence also increase. Aka, we should be able to walk and work any room, not because of what we wear, but *because of who we are*. I have never been more comfortable with strutting my not-so-flashy clothes then I am right now. Because I increasingly understand that my confidence, my love and my worth are not items in a Prada bag, but rooted and based in my heart, soul, and mind.

I hope and pray the utmost same for you: because you, my love, are an irreplaceable treasure.

> ***Note: I still love to dress up, but the reason why has changed dramatically, and I now do so more freely and with much greater joy.

> **#Growth Check**
>
> **Know when to Rest.** A busy life isn't always a productive one. What no one tells you is that rest is a *form* of productivity. Resting allows you to refresh yourself in God and life – especially through the stressful and not-so-promising days. Yes, today's world goes fast paced, but taking moments to slow down doesn't take you out of the race, it gives you the extra fuel to cross the finish line (in top form).
>
> When you feel like you're doing nothing, take that time to sit with God, delighting in Him. The best thing you can do for yourself is to spend time with the One who knows what successes are out there for you. Look to Him. Rest in Him.

Prayer Makes Things Happen

Dear Heavenly Father,

Thank You for this special time we share together. Even if it's only a few minutes, I know that a few minutes with You can mean more than a lifetime with anyone else. Thank You for taking charge of my life. I come to You today to ask that in a world of insecurities, help me defeat mine. You are so powerful and glorious that all that I should feel about myself is joy, reverence and honor. *Help me see what You see.* Let my confidence, joy and power be a direct reflection of You so that the world may know that all I have and have been given comes from You.

Your *loved* & *capable* daughter,

_____ (your name)

Amen

You are fearfully and wonderfully made.

Psalm 139:14a

The fruit of that righteousness will be peace; its effect will be quietness and confidence forever.

Isaiah 32:17

But blessed is the one who trusts in the LORD, whose confidence is in him.

Jeremiah 17:7

Being confident of this, that he who began a good work in you will carry it on to completion until the day of Christ Jesus.

Philippians 1:6

Get over yourself.

Goal #37: Get Rid of the Toxic

Day 37

More Joy, Less Stress

"To achieve great things, two things are needed: a plan and not quite enough time."
Leonard Bernstein

This has probably been the longest transition yet. I graduated with my master's and had been searching for jobs for over a year. No luck. One of the major things that stuck out was how I thought my purpose and self-worth would change during this job drought period. Previously mentioned, I was out of a job, moved away from a lot of my friends, and had no choice but to watch others succeed while I was still lost in transition. I try to be one hundred percent (100%) positive all the time, but I have to admit, I succumbed to the feelings of loneliness and sadness.

What do you do when you're stuck in a rut? You process those feelings and then → Get over yourself.

My most capable *Love*, I don't mean for that to sound harsh; but it's important to understand that *we haven't accomplished many of our goals because we are in our own way.* There will be times when joy is just around the corner, but we tend to choose every other option to stay down and disappointed.

The thoughts that once held me captive – EXHAUSTED me. The, "What am I going to do? Who do I turn to? All I've gotten is rejected. What good am I? No one cares. Where is ...." thoughts took over my mind, and I was always stressed and tapped out.

Insert therapy

Don't allow downs to cripple your growth. Yes, you may even be doing better than your peers in reaching your goals – or not. People may not think highly of you, or they might think you're phenomenal (which you are).

Whether others suffer, succeed, follow or lead is *none* of our business. The truth is *we are our own success story.* So rather than wasting time worrying what one is saying to the other, our persistent goal should be working on the better versions of ourselves – each day. Replace the worry with actively growing with God, and you'll find that joy gradually displaces what was once, overwhelming stress.

> **#GodandtheGoalDigger Check**
>
> **Bank over Bags:** You can dress for the job you want *without* breaking the bank. With the variety of shopping today, there are many outlets and stores that offer designer and non-designer clothes at more affordable prices. There is *Asos, Zara, Ross, TJ Maxx, Forever 21, H&M, JC Penney and Zaful*, to name a few. I often find myself getting to enjoy new designers when I "release" my care for wearing a particular brand. With every store, you can expect to do some screening to find your go-to outfits, and after finding your niche, focus on building up your bank account. *No bag is worth having nothing to carry.*

Prayer Makes Things Happen

Lord,

My plans are not Your plans. My plans are *not* Your plans. I thank You, that my plans are not Your plans. Because I know even the most conjured-up idea I have, cannot compare to all that You have for me. Please keep this drilled into me day after day. The standards that life sets are not Your standards. Help me to prioritize in a way that meets Your approval, and I ask that You bring balance to my life. When stress comes, remind me that I am not the strength of my circumstances. Remind me that You lighten my load when I come to You in need and want. In Your precious name.

Your *loved* & *capable* daughter,

_____ (your name)

Amen

A cheerful heart is good medicine.

Proverbs 17:22a (ASV)

No Challenge,
No Change.

Goal #38: Practice

Day 38

The Isolation of Moving On: The Hurt Habit

> *"Some of us think holding on makes us strong; but sometimes it is letting go."*
> **Hermann Hesse**

Don't be surprised when you're growing past hurt horizons to find people still on the shore. It takes people time to realize and accept a changing you – especially if they have not moved on themselves. Moving on and self-improvement, unfortunately, often leaves some people behind. Ideally, the goal is to uplift others and bring them with us, but one must be open and willing to come along.

When people who once impacted your life see you working on your joy – with or without their influence, it can be painful.

Hurt has a way of making itself comfortable. If we aren't careful, we can become so used to hurt that we forget what trust and joy look like.

As we've learned through this continued conversation, with every challenge, there is a lesson.

Today, hurt teaches us – *You are what you habituate:*

- A habit of resentment will breed more resentment and bitterness

But,

- A habit of *love, forgiveness* and *generosity* will breed growth and success.

Replace the not-so-positive practices with positive practices each day and *watch God work.* In His Scriptures, we know that God loves a cheerful giver (2 Corinthians 9:7), but He also *loves* a cheerful *thinker.* A joyful spirit makes way for blessings you never even thought possible. God reminds us that what we achieve depends on *what we believe.* What we believe starts with what and how we think. The great thing is this is the part you can control.

> **#Growth Check**
>
> **Have you dated yourself today?** The most important person you can get to know after God is you. We spend a lot of our lives denying who we are. Remember when we were kids and we would just DO? Then somewhere along the line, we learned what to do from what not to do. You ever take a minute to reassess that decision? Of course, we are forever thankful for the positive influences that helped make us who we are today. But just stop and ask yourself, are you achieving your full potential? If I listened to all those who said I was "too encouraging," I wouldn't be here encouraging millions of ladies to go get their faith and success.
>
> Take some time out to get to know yourself better. And then live it without fear.

Prayer Makes Things Happen

Lord,

Thank You for creating our emotions and thought systems. Though there are many ways to hurt, You've also said that there are even more ways to *heal*. I request something simple to ask but extraneous to do. Please help me to control my thoughts in a way that evokes positivity, prosperity

The Isolation of Moving On: The Hurt Habit

and Your perspective. Help me to understand that repeatedly staying in *The Hurt Habit* longer then You have planned for me will only keep me stagnant. I ask for Your hand in directing my new thoughts and direction. Thank You for this new beginning to Your wondrous blessings.

Your *loved* & *capable* daughter,

_____ (your name)

Amen

> *Each of you should give what you have decided in your heart to give, not reluctantly or under compulsion, for God **loves** a cheerful giver.*
>
> 2 Corinthians 9:7

> *Faith assures us of things **we expect** and convinces us of the existence of things we cannot see.*
>
> Hebrews 11:1 (GW)

> *Love is patient, love is kind. It does not envy, it does not boast, it is not proud. It does not dishonor others, it is not self-seeking, it is not easily angered, it keeps no record of wrongs. Love does not delight in evil but rejoices with the truth. It always protects, always trusts, always hopes, always perseveres. Love Never Fails.*
>
> 1 Corinthians 13:4-7

eal rest is often the most productive thing we can do.

Goal #39: Rejuvenate

Day 39

Unplug

"Being connected to everything has disconnected us from ourselves and the preciousness of this present moment."
L.M. Browning

[**Checks phone before writing this**]

I think it's safe to say that we spend considerably, large amounts of time on our phones, computers: basically anything technology. Since the age of social media and networking, there is much to gain from these venues. Technology is a wonderful thing – except when it isn't. The increase in technological advances has enabled us, ALWAYS, to be accessible. While beneficial, one of the hardest aspects of being so readily available is learning how to press our own "off" button.

We may sleep, but I find that fewer and fewer people actually *rest*. Though sleeping can be a form of rest, when we lie and wake to a million thoughts in our minds – all at once, the idea of rest goes out the window. And I know – we are all busy bosses. But even the smallest uninterrupted rest can add extra hours of energy to your upcoming week.

For me, rest is defined as something or an action that takes your mind off the day: leaving you *more refreshed* than before. With that in mind, rest can be going on an unrelated-to-work outing with friends or something like laying without purpose. Some of my most energizing times come from the *"simple lay."*

My simple lay consists of maybe five (5) – twenty (20) minutes of just sitting/laying and being. When thoughts come into my head, I just let them go on their natural path, without interfering with any current views or preparations of plans. It allows me to process and catch up with my sometimes mile-a-minute schedule. Though the simple lay may not be your rest refresher, I encourage you to find something that revitalizes you, venturing your way to enjoying life rather than just living in it.

> **#GodandtheGoalDigger Check**
>
> I'm pretty sure you're not convinced this is a Goal Digger move - **Rest:**
>
> God rested on the seventh day, not because He had to – He's God. He rested on the seventh day to set an example for us to follow: that constant going, without stopping to enjoy the moments He's given us is *not* how He made us to live. While the drive to financial freedom is warranted, one of God's biggest proclamations in His Word is to rest in Him - depend on Him - *count on Him*. The sad thing is that society wants you to believe that when you take time out to spend with God, you are doing "nothing" - when that is the furthest thing from the truth. The secret is and has always been: spend time with God → depend on Him → He grants you success.
>
> Make up your mind to rest and enjoy the now and what is to come.

Prayer Makes Things Happen

Dear Lord,

Thank You for today. Even as I pray right now, the phone is going off, and something else needs to be done. But that's life. Please help me to find a

Unplug

way to unplug from everything else completely. You even rested on the 7th day of life to set the example for us that rest is essential. For whatever "me time" I can make or receive, I ask that You optimize it as only You can. Help 2 minutes feel like 2 hours – I want to give my heart and time to You.

Your *loved* & *capable* daughter,

_____ (your name)

Amen

> *Then Jesus said, "Come to me, all of you who are weary and carry heavy burdens, and I will give you rest. Take my yoke upon you. Let me teach you, because I am humble and gentle at heart, and you will give rest for your souls. For my yoke is easy to bear, and the burden I give you is light.*
>
> Matthew 11:28-30

What people don't get is that if we **really** lived the way God intended us to, everyone would want a piece of the action.

Goal #40: Growth

Day 40

God and The Professional

"You cannot believe in God until you believe in yourself."
Swami Vivekananda

Is it and? Is it either-or? A lot of the times we think that articulating God through our work is minimizing it, or even as far as belittling our appearance in the professional realm. Love? This mindset is a stumbling block every Goal Digger has or will cross. On the one hand, we'd like to praise God for His blessings all day, every day, everywhere. On the other (left hand if you were wondering), we don't want to: 1) offend anyone; 2) turn people away because they may believe in something different.

Another Perspective:

We all have beliefs. They are reflected in our fashion attire, cooking style(s), and choice of people we befriend, to name a few. If we showcase those aspects of our lives more than what we say really fuels our drive and commitment to life (in this case, God) – *something doesn't add up!*

NO, I don't mean you have to put up a God post every day out of the week. There is a time and a place for everything. I'm asking you (as I ask myself every morning), what does God mean to you? If you see God just as someone you go to when you need help, then it makes sense that we would only hear about Him in dire situations. But if you are on the path to seek His will, depend on Him as the fuel to your faith, and see the many joys in this life as His blessings, then that should readily be apparent to others as well.

As a fellow #GoalDigger, the word "entrepreneurship" already gives us both goosebumps. I'm pretty sure your media feed had a cameo or two of the following hashtags: #goaldigger #GirlBoss, #getit, #goalgetter, #bossmoves, #dontsleeponme, #imabouttogooff.

Okay, maybe not the last one.

But in some shape or form, we are showcasing our belief in the Goal Digger realm. Similarly, if our goal with God is to follow Him and be the best example He has brought us to be, then somewhere along the line, our beliefs should be represented and readily seen.

Last Thing

When God says He forgives us, He forgives us wholeheartedly, but He also adds that He forgives us when we forgive others (Matthew 6:14-15). Likewise, when God says He represents us without worry or shame, He asks for us to represent Him in the same way. It also doesn't hurt to know that the people we strive to be: The Denzel Washington's, Carrie Underwood's, Yvonne Orji's, Tim Tebow's, Will Smith's, etc., openly share their faith in God time and time again.

#Growth Check

Take a look at all of the days, your listening prayers and your circle proclamations and just reflect where God has taken you in these past few weeks.

Thank Him for all He has revealed and all that He will continue to disclose in the future.

Prayer Makes Things Happen

Dear Heavenly Father,

I have prayed and thanked You for the time during this book adventure, and I have seen Your work in and around me. For what I have not seen yet, keep me in faith and trust, knowing that what I truly believe in will come to fruition. Help my belief to stay in You. Through whatever trials, I ask that You will remain alongside me as You have done these past 40 days.

I proclaim Your health, wealth, purpose, passion, love, blessings and all that is to come for me and my sisters in Christ reading with me across the world. Help me to get so excited about You and our relationship that I can easily share Your goodness and wonder with others. This is *definitely not* a goodbye, but more a rubric on how I want to continue to proceed life: with You at the top, taking care of me – every single day.

Your *loved* & *capable* daughter,

_____ (your name)

Amen

> *Whatever you have learned or received or heard from me, or seen in me—put it into practice. And the God of peace will be with you.*
>
> **Philippians 4:9**
>
> *Commit your work to the Lord, and your plans will be established.*
>
> **Proverbs 16:3**

Circle For Success

This is it! Now that we have completed all the circle sections in this book: it's time to put them together. You have set the groundwork for how to pray on different aspects of your life, thoroughly and powerfully. Yay you!

Don't stop here, Love. *Keep Dreaming. Keep Doing. Keep Going. Keep Growing. Keep Praying. Keep Circling.* You are nothing short of a masterpiece! God is and will continue to work miracles on your behalf. Continue to go to Him with confidence and humility – and watch God work in, through and for you.

Love, it has been my absolute pleasure sharing these 40 days of self-discovery and intention. I would love to hear from you! You can find my contact information on the back cover of this book. Until then, May God always provide you with the utmost blessings overflow!

Look back at what you filled in for your success circles (on Days 5, 10, 15, 20, 25, 30 & 35) and fill them in below!

The Core

Health

Physical

Financial

Emotional

Spiritual

Mental

Have you ever seen a flower emerge from concrete? It may look delicate on the outside, but when it grows – it can break through virtually anything. And that's a flower!

Imagine all the more you can do.

-Adria Bee

#GodandtheGoalDigger Check

Putting it together: After your last reflection and compilation of your prayer circles, *make a copy* and place it somewhere you can see daily so that you can look back and continuously pray over your specific goals. W*atch* God take you to new heights in your journey; I am SO proud of you! You are about to embark upon greatness, Love. Get ready for your blessing.!

Closing Prayer

Dear Almighty Father,

Thank You for being with me through each and every day of this book journey. Through the ups, the downs and the in-betweens of life I thank You that everything has its purpose. I am starting to realize that living like I have control of my life will never leave me entirely fulfilled if it's a life that You didn't plan for me. I ask that You become the control and the leader of my life. Help me know when it's Your voice speaking to me and when to act accordingly. I pray that I will keep learning and growing in faith and what I can do if I just believe in You. Thank You for reminding me of how awesome I am – fearfully and wonderfully! Thank You for Your promises to always be with me, to love me unconditionally and to know me wholeheartedly – even when I don't know myself. I place my trust in You this and every day.

Your *loved* & *capable* daughter,

_____ (your name)

Amen

For we are God's handiwork, created in Christ Jesus to do good works, which God prepared in advance for us to do.

Ephesians 3:20

For I am not ashamed of the gospel, because it is the power of God that brings salvation to everyone who believes.

Romans 1:16

This may be the end of this book,

but your story has just begun.

Praying for your continued blessings overflow,

Adria Bee

About the Author

Adria Bee, also known as Adria B. McCardy, has a master's degree in Communication. She is the *Co-founder* and *Creative Director* of Color Me Reading Productions and *Brooke & Lee* ([www.brookeandlee.com,](www.brookeandlee.com) itsadriabee@gmail.com).

She has a great love for people, her family, faith, friends and her home country, The Bahamas. Along with her venture and Marketing Manager day job, clients also may know her as their local insurance agent, photographer, branding coach, creative director, writer and/or social media consultant. With an entrepreneurial mindset and a jack of all trades' pursuit, her goal is to inspire love and positivity to everyone she encounters. One of her most current, personal mottoes is "Watch God, not people," but her all-time favorite quote comes from Maya Angelou: "… people will forget what you said, people will forget what you did, but people will never forget how you made them feel."

Titles Related to the Author

- *Mr. Friend* – by Brooke** & Lee
- *Dave the Brave* – by Brooke & Lee
- *Crayons and Colors* – by Brooke & Lee
- *Where da Conch Gone?* – by Brooke & Lee
- *Little Hands Praying God's Wisdom for My Family* – by Hope McCardy, with Lisa Bastian and Brooke & Lee
- *Little Hands Praying God's Wisdom for My Friends* – by Hope McCardy, with Lisa Bastian and Brooke & Lee
- *Little Hands Praying God's Wisdom for Myself* – by Hope McCardy, with Lisa Bastian and Brooke & Lee
- *Be Prepared* – by Hope McCardy, with Lisa Bastian and Brooke & Lee
- *Share Save Spend* – by Hope McCardy and Brooke & Lee
- *The Legend of the Flaming Dragon* – by Rashad McCardy
- *31 Days of Praying God's Wisdom for Myself* – by Hope McCardy

- *31 Days of Praying God's Wisdom for My Husband* – by Hope McCardy

- *31 Days of Praying God's Wisdom for My Children* – by Hope McCardy

- *Be Blessed and Encouraged* – by Hope McCardy

**"Brooke" is one of the pen names of the *God & the GOAL Digger* author, Adria Bee. She comes from a family of authors (including her sister Kristi "Lee" McCardy) who all believe in God and His everlasting love and power.

References

Batterson, M. (2012). *Draw the Circle: The 40 Day Prayer Challenge* (11.9.2012 edition). Grand Rapids, Mich: Zondervan.

Batterson, M. (2016). *The Circle Maker: Praying Circles Around Your Biggest Dreams and Greatest Fears* (Expanded edition). Zondervan.

Geegh, M. (2014). *God Guides - Listening to God for His Guidance*. Retrieved from https://god-guides.com/

Warren, R. (2019). Daily Hope with Rick Warren - Devotional. Retrieved from https://pastorrick.com/devotional/

Zondervan. (2012). *NIV, Women's Devotional Bible, Hardcover* (Special edition). Grand Rapids, Michigan: Zondervan.